BOOK 1

READING
with
UNDERSTANDING
a comprehension course

JOHN SEELY

OXFORD UNIVERSITY PRESS 1983

Oxford University Press, Walton Street, Oxford OX2 6DP

Oxford   London   Glasgow
New York   Toronto   Melbourne   Auckland
Kuala Lumpur   Singapore   Hong Kong   Tokyo
Delhi   Bombay   Calcutta   Madras   Karachi
Nairobi   Dar es Salaam   Cape Town

and associated companies in
Beirut   Berlin   Ibadan   Mexico City   Nicosia

Oxford is a trade mark of Oxford University Press

ISBN 0 19 831140 0

Also by John Seely:

Oxford Secondary English

Book 1   0 19 831133 8   Teacher's Book 1   0 19 831134 6
Book 2   0 19 831135 4   Teacher's Book 2   0 19 831136 2
Book 3   0 19 831137 0   Teacher's Book 3   0 19 831138 9

Dramakit   0 19 913238 0

Playkits   0 19 913259 3

In Context   0 19 913222 4

Typeset in Great Britain by
Rowland Phototypesetting Ltd, Bury St Edmunds, Suffolk
Printed in Great Britain by
Pitman Press Ltd, Bath

CONTENTS

ACKNOWLEDGEMENTS

The publishers would like to thank the following for permission to reprint copyright material

J. & A. Ahlberg: from 'The Sad Case of Thomas Tull' from *The Vanishment of Thomas Tull* (1977). Reprinted by permission of A. & C. Black Publishers Ltd. **Nigel Baguley:** 'Hurricane Tracey' from *Natural Disasters* (1979). Reprinted by permission of Harrap Ltd. **Gun** and **Ingvar Bjork:** from *Bees* (1977). Reprinted by permission of Pelham Books Ltd. **Judy Blume:** 'An Addition to the Family' from *Superfudge* (1980). Reprinted by permission of The Bodley Head. **Lucy M. Boston:** Extract from *The Fossil Snake* (1975). Reprinted by permission of The Bodley Head. **Edward Boyd:** 'Grace Darling' from *The Noel Streatfield Summer Holiday Book* (Dent 1973). **V. Carrick:** 'The Wily Hare' from *Tales of Wise and Foolish Animals* (Dover 1969). **Charles Causley:** 'King Mark of Cornwall' from *The Last King of Cornwall* (Hodder & Stoughton 1978). Reprinted by permission of David Higham Associates Limited. **Alan Coren:** 'Dan Dundee and the Dusty D' from *Buffalo Arthur* (1976). Reprinted by permission of Robson Books, London. **J. Curry:** from *How Did It Start* (1977). Reprinted by permission of The Hamlyn Publishing Group Limited. **Tim Healey:** from *Timespan, Escapes* (1979) © Macdonald Education Limited. Reprinted by permission of Macdonald & Co. (Publishers) Ltd. **A. Henley:** from *A Family Talking*. Reprinted by permission of A. & C. Black Publishers Ltd. **Ted Hughes:** from *How the Whale Became* (1973). Reprinted by permission of Faber & Faber Ltd. **A. Jack:** from *UFO's* (1979). Reprinted by permission of Franklin Watts Ltd. **Gene Kemp:** 'Ten Pound Note' from *The Turbulent Term of Tyke Tiler* (1977). Reprinted by permission of Faber & Faber Ltd. **George Layton:** 'The Balaclava Story' from *A Northern Childhood: The Balaclava Story and Other Stories* (Knockouts Series). Reprinted by permission of Longman Group Ltd. **David Line:** from *Run For Your Life*. Reprinted by permission of Jonathan Cape Ltd., for the author. **Ruth Manning-Sanders:** 'The Lion in the Sewer' from *Animal Stories* (Oxford University Press 1961). Reprinted by permission of David Higham Associates Ltd. **Chris Rawling:** from *Daredevils & Scaredycats* (1979). Reprinted by permission of Abelard-Schuman Ltd. **James Reeves:** from *Fables From Aesop* (1961). Reprinted by permission of Blackie & Son Ltd. **C. Schenk:** from *Jubilee Terrace* (1979). Reprinted by permission of A. & C. Black Publishers Ltd. **Colin Thiele:** from *Storm-boy*. Reprinted by permission of the author and Rigby Publishers. **E. & C. Turner:** from *Bats* (1974). Reprinted by permission of Wayland Publishers Ltd. **Laura Ingalls Wilder**: from *The Little House on the Prairie* (Méthuen 1937). Reprinted by permission of Associated Book Publishers Ltd. **Brian Williams:** from *Conquerors of Everest* (Kingfisher Books). Reprinted by permission of Grisewood and Dempsey Ltd.

Every effort has been made to trace and contact copyright holders but this has not always been possible. We apologize for any infringement of copyright.

The publishers would like to thank the following for permission to reproduce photographs:

Barnaby's Picture Library, pp. 9, 25, 86; Camera Press, pp. 17, 54, 81, 86, 88; Fortean Picture Library, p. 13; Frank Lane, p. 41; Richard and Sally Greenhill, p. 65; Mansell Collection, p. 76; Network, p. 62; E. North, p. 21; J. Thomas, pp. 5, 58; John Topham, pp. 36, 45; Zoological Society of London, p. 49.

Illustrations by: Norma Burgin, Peter Branfield, John Taylor, Krystyna Turska.

1 TEN POUND NOTE

Section A   The money

In this section ten words have been missed out. There is a list of them underneath.

☐ Read the passage.

☐ Work out which word should go in which space.

☐ Write down the number of the space and the word that should go in it.

We'd gone right through the —1— collecting the teachers' tea —2— and had got to the canteen door when Danny waved the ten pound note at me. It took me a —3— of minutes to —4— what it was, 'cos it looked highly unlikely in Danny's grimy mitt. Then I —5— him into the canteen, sure to be —6— on a Friday afternoon at five to three. The pandemonium of a —7— school playtime died away, and we could —8— the rain drumming on the roof instead.

'Where didja —9— that, you nutter?'

'Out of Bonfire's purse. She'd left it —10—. On the desk. So I took it. No one saw me, Tyke.'

pushed   couple   money   open   realize   school   get   empty   wet
hear

Section B   A problem

☐ Read the passage carefully and then answer the questions that follow it.

I shook him.

'Don't you see? Don't you understand, you idiotic imbecile?' I shouted. Before he could reply the buzzer went for the end of play, so I headed for our classroom, 4M, with Danny running sideways trying to talk to me.

'Why you all mad, Tyke? Don't be mad at me, Tyke.'

I didn't answer.

'I got it for you. I want you to have half of it. You can buy anything you like, Tyke.'

I took no notice. He pulled at my arm. I shook him off.

'Get knotted.'

'Tyke. Tyke?'

We reached the classroom. I pushed Danny into the book corner.

'Listen Danny. Don't you see? Don't you understand? You can't spend it, because they'll ask you where you got it from, and they won't believe what you say, and they'll want to ask your mum, and then you'll be for it.'

His face went sad, like my dog at home when she's caught raiding the dustbins. She can't stop doing it, but she has terrible sorrow when anyone catches her. Danny's the same, though it's money with him, not dustbins.

'It's no use, Danny boyo. You can't keep it.'

'I didn't think.'

'You never do, do you? Now go and give it back to Bonfire.'

Red colour ran all over his face, then flowed away, leaving it white. He began to tremble.

'I can't do that. You know the row I got into last time.'

'I'll take it back to her.'

'Oh, no. They'll know it was me what pinched it.'

'Just what are we going to do with it, then? Play Monopoly with it? Stick it up on the wall?'

'Hide it, and put it back later.'

'You must be joking!'

'Please, Tyke. You do it. You're clever. You can do anything.'

'Gee, t'anks!'

1   When was the conversation taking place?
2   What mood was Tyke in?
3   Why did Tyke say that Danny could not keep the money?
4   How did Danny feel about that?
5   What did Tyke tell him to do?
6   What effect did this have on Danny?
7   What did Tyke offer to do?
8   Why did Danny think this was no good?
9   What was Danny's solution to the problem?
10   What did Tyke think of that?

Section C   Escape

This section has been divided into seven parts. Except for the beginning, the parts have been printed in the wrong order.

☐ Study them carefully and work out the order they should be in.

☐ Write the numbers in the correct order.

I would've said more, but Sir came in, and the noise died down. Sir is Mr William Merchant, and he's all right. The end of Friday afternoon is ours to do what we like, make our own choice.

1   'Can I take the tea money to the office, please, Sir?'
       'Yes, Tyke.'

2   For everybody but me, that is. As far as I could see I didn't have any choice. For any minute now, Bonfire would find out that she'd been robbed, and then along would come Chief Sir, the Headmaster, and we'd be searched.

3   'Nothing, sir.'
     'You look a bit green. Got a pain?'
     I thought I heard voices outside.

4   It's happened before. And so, before it happened again, I'd got to get this nasty bit of brown paper from under my sweater and stowed away somewhere safe, till I could put it back in Bonfire's bag. I went up to the desk.

5   I suddenly felt sure the note was slipping. I held where I thought it was with one hand, the tea tin in the other.
     'Anything the matter?'

6   'No, sir.' I headed for the door as fast as possible to be out of the room before the searchers arrived.

Section D   Writing

Do you think Tyke succeeds? What do you think happens?

Write the continuation of the story, describing what Tyke does with the ten pound note and what happens in the end.

2 AESOP'S FABLES

Section A   Birdcatcher and partridge

Ten words have been missed out from this story. They are included in the list at the end, together with ten other words that do not belong to the story.

☐ Read the story and choose suitable words to fill the blanks.

☐ Write the number of each blank and beside it write the word you have chosen.

Peter was a birdcatcher. He used to go out with his nets and —1— them cunningly among the bushes, so that —2— in search of food would get caught in them. Then he would kill them and —3— them in the market. One day he caught a fat partridge. The bird cried out

9

—4— and spoke to Peter.

'Oh Mr Birdcatcher, I beg you to let me go. I never did you any harm. Oh, —5— my life, I beg you!'

'I don't know so much about that,' said Peter. 'Why —6— I let you go, eh?'

'If you will spare my life,' answered the partridge, 'I might be useful to you. I can sit beside your net and —7— other birds into it. As you know, birds of a feather flock together; and many young partridges will I —8— into your snare.'

'Why, you miserable traitor!' cried Peter scornfully. 'I might have let you go, but now I shall do no such thing. No —9— deserves to live who is cowardly enough to save his own skin by betraying his —10—.'

Moral: only a coward betrays his fellows

animals   sell   release   drop   should   aloud   must   lay piteously   attract   take   bring   send   enemies   animal   lead creature   spare   friends   birds

---

Section B   Lion, goat, and vulture

☐ Read the story carefully and then answer the questions that follow.

It was a hot day. Lion and Goat were both thirsty, but the pool was small. Goat bent down his head to drink, when Lion came up beside him and growled fiercely. 'I shall drink first,' he said. 'I am King of All the Animals, and it is my right. Get out of my way!'

'No,' said the Goat, 'I shall drink first. I found the water. You can wait till I have finished.'

'You'll drink it all up,' said the Lion. 'There's not very much left, and I am nearly dead with thirst.'

'And I haven't had a drop all day,' answered Goat.

So they quarrelled. Lion chased Goat to the top of a great rock, and, hot as he was, Goat bounded out of the way. Neither of them was able to drink in peace.

Suddenly Lion stopped chasing Goat and looked up into the hot blue sky. Goat looked too. There, circling slowly above them, was Vulture. All the animals knew and feared him. He is the Bird of Death, who waits to pounce on the bodies of dead animals and eat their flesh. Lion and Goat knew, both at once, that if they did not stop fighting, they would die of thirst, and Vulture would pluck their bodies to the bone.

'If we go on quarrelling,' said Lion, 'we shall both die of thirst, and that will be the end of us. Go to the water and drink, but don't take it all!'

Goat did as he was told, and the two animals quenched their thirst instead of fighting.

1 Why did Lion think he should drink first?
2 Why did Goat think he should drink first?
3 Why was Lion unwilling to wait until Goat had drunk?
4 What was Vulture doing?
5 What was he waiting for?
6 What did Lion and Goat do when they saw Vulture?
7 What do you think is the moral of this fable?

Section C Oak and reed

In this section six sentences, or parts of sentences have been missed out.

☐ Read the story through and try to work out what you think they must have been. Of course, you won't be able to guess the exact words that were there, but think of what could be put in so that the story makes sense.

☐ Write the number of each blank and beside it the words that you think should go there.

A great oak tree stood on a hill, and a slender reed grew at its foot. When the wind blew, the reed swayed and shook, ——————— ————1———————————.

The tree looked down at the little reed and called to him:

'Why do you tremble so when the wind blows? Why don't you keep still, like me?'

'I'm not as strong as you,' said the reed in his small piping voice. '———————————2———————————.'

'Then you must be a coward,' said the oak scornfully, 'and a poor sort of plant. You should learn to stand up for yourself. ——— ——————3——————.'

And the oak stood on the hill, taller and stronger than ever. ——————————4——————————. A mighty wind blew from off the sea and made a terrible roaring, so that people said that they had never heard a gale like this one in all their lives. The oak

stood firm and the slender reed bowed before the wind until it
touched the ground. ———————————5———————————,
and when in the morning it ceased, the reed stood up again, but the
oak lay flat on the ground, ———————————6———————————
————.

**Moral: the proud will be destroyed, but the humble will outlive
their misfortunes.**

Section D   Writing

Make up a fable to illustrate one of these morals:
1   Look before you leap.
2   Pride goes before a fall.
3   Good looks aren't everything.
4   In good times prepare for when the bad times come.
5   It doesn't pay to be too clever.

3 UFOs

Section A How it all started

In this section ten words have been missed out.

☐ Read the section carefully and try to work out what the missing words should be.

☐ Write down the number of each blank and beside it write the word you have chosen.

People have claimed to have seen strange objects in the sky for hundreds of —1—. But the first sighting of a 'flying saucer' was in 1947. —2— than 10,000 sightings have been notified and investigated since people began to keep —3— in 1949.

One day in June 1947 Kenneth Arnold took off in his small —4—.
He was flying over mountains in Washington State. Suddenly, he
—5— a strange sight. He saw nine silver discs flying in formation at a
very high speed. They had no wings, and they reflected the sun like
—6—. These strange discs wove in and out between the mountain
peaks, and then —7— very quickly.

When Arnold landed, he —8— what he had seen to newsmen.
He told them that he had seen objects which 'flew like —9— would if
you skipped them across water'. The next day American newspapers
reported the story, and gave these peculiar —10— the name 'flying
saucers'.

Section B   What people think

☐ Read the section through and then answer the questions that follow
it.

A flying saucer is usually called a UFO. UFO is short for 'unidentified
flying object'. A UFO is a flying object which cannot be explained.

Have you ever seen a UFO? Do you believe they exist? In 1977
fifty-six per cent of the population in the United States said they
believed in UFOs. Eleven per cent of the population said they had
seen a UFO.

Are people who see and report UFOs strange? Do they also see
ghosts and spirits? Do they just imagine they are seeing UFOs?

The answer to these questions seems to be 'no'. People who report
sightings are usually sensible and sane. They have almost always
seen *something*. They make reports because they are worried or
curious about what they have seen.

Early one morning in April 1966 a UFO was spotted by two Ohio
State policemen. It came out of some woods and went towards their
parked car. As the UFO came nearer, it got brighter and brighter.
When it was over the policemen it was as big as a house. It made a
strange humming noise. The two policemen were very frightened
and ran to their car for protection.

The UFO moved off and the policemen began to follow it. They
chased it for 40 miles at speeds of up to 100 m.p.h. They finally
stopped by the side of another police car. The four policemen
watched as the bright shape went straight up into the sky and
disappeared.

Some of the statements that follow are true. Some are false.

☐ Read them carefully. Decide which are true and which are false.

☐ Write down the numbers and, against each one, write *True* or *False* .

1 UFOs cannot be explained.
2 In 1977 56% of Americans believed in UFOs.
3 In 1977 fewer than 10% of Americans said that they had seen a UFO.
4 People who say that they have seen a UFO are usually mad.
5 When the Ohio policemen first saw the UFO they were not in their car.
6 The UFO they saw was silent.
7 It travelled at over 90 mph.
8 In the end it climbed rapidly and disappeared.

Section C   More sightings

In this section five sentences have been blanked out. The missing sentences are printed at the end of the section, but they are in the wrong order.

☐ Read the passage through and decide which sentence should go in which blank.

☐ Write down the number of each blank and against it the letter of the sentence you have chosen.

In October 1969 Governor Jimmy Carter (who became President Carter in 1976) reported seeing a UFO. He said, 'It was shortly after dark, and ten or twelve men all watched it. It seemed to move towards us, then a bit away, then return, then depart. ————1 ————————. Luminous, but not solid.'

Captain Denis Wood had been a pilot with British Airways for twenty years. One day in July 1976, when he was flying over Portugal, he looked out of his window and saw something appear in the west. It was a round, brilliant, bright white object. ————2 ————————. Captain Wood decided that it was not a satellite, not a balloon and not a star. ————3———————. Suddenly, they saw two cigar-shaped objects come out of nothing. ————4 ————————. After eight minutes they took off at a very high speed and disappeared. This sighting was reported also by two other pilots who were flying in the same area that day.

The people who made these reports were not crazy. They were not imagining things. —————5————— . The question to ask is 'What was it that they saw?'

a)   They were big and solid, and gave off their own light.
b)   It came between the plane and the sun.
c)   It was bluish, then reddish.
d)   They did see *something*.
e)   His crew watched the bright light, too.

Section D   Writing

Make up a story about yourself seeing a UFO. Tell it in one of these forms:

1   As a newspaper report. 'Local girl (or boy) sights UFO.'
2   As a conversation with a friend who doesn't believe you.
3   As an interview with a TV news reporter.

4 JUBILEE TERRACE

Section A The houses

In this section ten words have been missed out.

☐ Read the passage and work out what you think the missing words should be.

☐ Write down the numbers of the blanks. Write the word you have chosen beside each number.

Jubilee Terrace has been standing for quite a long time. Like every street, it has a —1— to tell. Children have been born here. They have played in the street. They have grown up and gone out to work. They have got married and had children of their —2—.

The houses in Jubilee Terrace are quite small. They've got three —3—. In the old days many people had large families. It was quite common to have seven children and there was even one family with seventeen.

It must have been quite a —4— for a big family to live in one of these houses. There wasn't room for —5— to have a bed. Usually the mother and father would sleep in one bedroom. Another would have all the girls sleeping —6— in one bed. The boys would share a bed in the third bedroom.

One man had such a big family that there wasn't any room for him to sleep in his own —7—. He had to get a job working nights, so that he could have a bed to sleep in during the day.

Of course with so many people —8— in a small space, there was a lot of housework. There was lots of cooking to do, and washing up. There were many clothes to wash and —9—, and it was a hard job to keep the house clean and tidy. The children were given jobs to help with the housework.

For instance one of the older girls would empty the —10— out of the grate every morning. The younger children ran errands when they came home from school.

Section B   Lights and baths

☐ Read the sentences and then answer the questions that follow them.

a)   When these old people were young, there wasn't any electricity in Jubilee Terrace.
b)   There are still gas lamps in one of the houses.
c)   All the houses used to have gas lamps.
d)   You can't just press a switch and get some light.
e)   You have to open a gas tap and strike a match and light the lamp carefully, making sure you don't break the mantle.
f)   There were gas lamps in the street as well.
g)   Every night, when it got dark, a man had to come round with a light on the end of a long pole so that he could reach up to light the street lamps.
h)   The boys and girls took it in turns to have baths.
i)   One night all the girls had to go to bed early.
j)   The tub was filled with hot water from the boiler.
k)   One of the boys got in and was scrubbed clean.
l)   While he dried, one of his brothers got into the same water.

m) It took too long to heat water for everyone to have a clean tubful.
n) Next night it would be the girls' turn and the boys would have to go to bed early.
o) There was only one tap in the sink – a cold one.
p) If you wanted hot water you had to heat it in a boiler.
q) This took quite a long time over a coal fire.

☐ Write down the letters of all the sentences that tell you about each of the following topics:

1 Gas
2 Having a bath
3 How gas lamps were lit
4 Why gas lamps made more work than electricity
5 How water was heated
6 How the boys used to have a bath

☐ Write one or more complete sentences to answer each of these questions.

1 Explain how gas lamps were lit.
2 Why was gas less convenient than electricity?
3 How did they heat water to have a bath?
4 Describe how bath night was organized.

Section C Food

In this section a lot of words have been missed out. Only the key words have been left.

☐ Read them carefully and work out what the full sentences should be.

☐ Then write your own version of the passage, using the words that are printed and filling in the gaps so that the sentences make sense.

People didn't have electric cookers ——————— many ———————
didn't ——————— have ——————— gas ring. ——————— did ———
—— cooking ——————— coal fire.
    Just by ——————— fire ——————— metal stand ——————— hob.
You ——————— swing ——————— towards ——————— heat ———
—— put ——————— saucepan ——————— kettle on it. ———————
usually ——————— kettle whistling away on the hob.
    ——————— Sunday ——————— buy ——————— dinner ———
—— corner shop. ——————— could have rabbit, potatoes, carrots,
turnips and onions, all ——————— few pennies.

During ———— week ———— food wasn't so good. Sometimes ———— had 'rattle in the pan'. ———— potatoes, bacon
and onions fried ———— frying pan ———— bit of water.
———— never enough ———— so ———— rattle.
When ———— anything left over, ———— put ————
'see pie' ———— meant 'wait and see pie'. You never knew
———— underneath ———— pastry.

Section D Writing

Read through sections A,B,C again and think about the changes that
have taken place since the days of Jubilee Terrace. Decide whether
you would have liked to live in those days, or if you really prefer life
today. Write down your feelings and the reasons for them.

5 A FAMILY TALKING

In this unit four members of a London family talk about themselves.
They are:
Lemuel, the father
Daphne, the mother
Lawrence, the elder son, aged 16
Monica, the elder daughter, aged 13½

Section A Running

In this section ten words have been missed out.

☐ Read the passage and work out what you think the missing words
should be.

☐ Write the number of each blank and, against each one, write the word you have chosen.

Lawrence: I love sport – all kinds. I run and play football and do athletics for Middlesex. And I play basketball for the Ealing schools.

When I start off in a race I'm dead —1—, wondering if I'm going to win or not. Then the —2— goes and I set off and I've got about 150 yards to go. I can —3— someone coming up behind me and I push and push and push. You have to explode yourself. And if the —4— bloke's still on you, you keep pushing and —5— yourself to go.

You just run on and there's only 20 yards to go, 10 yards, you're still in front, —6— your neck out – and you win! And then you look back and you say 'Easy, easy,' but at the —7— it was really hard.

Monica: I like running too. I used to get —8— of Lawrence, you see. He used to run a lot and win —9— and things, so I started trying and now I win medals and things too. We still race each other —10—, but he wins.

Section B   Work

In this section five sentences have been missed out. The missing sentences are listed at the end of the passage, but they are in the wrong order.

☐ Read the passage and decide which sentence should fill which blank.

☐ Write down the number of each blank and against it write the letter of the sentence you have chosen.

Lemuel: I came to England in 1959 just before Daphne and I got married. When I first got here I saw the houses, so small and grey, and I thought 'What's this?' ————————1—————————
————. I said 'Look at all those factories, so many factories; getting jobs in this place *must* be easy!'

————————2———————————. People used to come to me and say 'Look, I want a cabinet,' or something, and I would build them one.

When I first came here I got a woodworking job in a factory, but it was boring – one type of work all the time, fixing drawers. ————
————————3—————————.

Then I went to work in the packing department of another factory. That was better because I didn't have to stick to just one thing. I

had responsibility there. Then I went to another factory where I had to work night shifts sometimes. But after that I started full time with the church, and that's where I am now. ——————————4——
————————————————.

Daphne: From the beginning I always wanted to be a teacher. I started off taking exams when I was young, but I failed them. I was a bit of a loggerhead. Then I went on to do dressmaking. I didn't like it at all – I hated it. ——————————5——————————. Wages were very low in those days.

Mind you, when I came here and started having children I was glad I had learnt because I managed to make a lot of clothes for them and I made my own things as well.

Now I'm a secretary in a college and I have to work very hard there, so I'm often tired when I get home.

a) In Jamaica I did carpentry.
b) In fact the first thing in England that caught my eye was the chimneys on top of the houses.
c) It's very interesting, but it keeps me very busy.
d) It was all mass production, it wasn't creative.
e) I worked for a dressmaker in Kingston.

Section C   Jamaica

☐ Read the passage and then answer the questions.

Daphne: Out in Jamaica you get all sorts of different vegetables: plantain, coconuts, breadfruit, sweet potatoes and things. We used to grow all our own vegetables there. We never had to buy any.

Over here I can't buy all those things easily, so I usually buy English vegetables. I sometimes buy West Indian vegetables as a special treat for the family, but they're very expensive and they have come all the way from the West Indies, so they aren't fresh any more.

There's a shop round the corner where I buy most of our food. I often send Lloyd and Pauline down there to get something for me.

Lawrence: I went to the West Indies with Mum five years ago, and we stayed with our relations. They live inland on a farm.

I like to hear the way some of the people talk there. They talk Patois,* which is different from English. Monica and I are trying to learn it. We speak it with our friends at school. Mum and Dad spoke Patois and English before they came to England, but they speak English most of the time now. They weren't allowed to speak Patois

* Patois is also called Creole.

when they were at school and they don't much like us speaking it now.

In Jamaica I spoke it with my relations, but sometimes I didn't understand because they speak so fast. When I speak fast I make lots of mistakes and get muddled up and I sound so stupid.

Monica: I went to the West Indies too, but I got a bit homesick.

1 Make a list of the different vegetables people can buy in Jamaica.
2 Why didn't Daphne buy vegetables when she lived in Jamaica?
3 Why are these vegetables not so good when she buys them in England?
4 When Lawrence went to the West Indies where did he stay?
5 What language do he and his relatives speak as well as English?
6 Which language does Lawrence speak better?
7 How did Monica feel on her visit to the West Indies?

Section D   Writing

1 Choose one of the members of the family. Write a paragraph about him or her. Use the facts given in the unit, but use your own words as far as possible.
2 The passages used in this unit were written down from tape recorded interviews with the family.
   a) What do you think were the questions that were asked? Make a list of them.
   b) Suppose you were going to interview the members of a family about their way of life, what questions would you ask them? Make a list of them.

6 HOW DID IT START?

Section A   Cat's eyes

In this section ten words have been missed out.

☐ Read the section and think of suitable words to fill the spaces.

☐ Write the number of each space and write the word you have chosen beside each number.

Forty years ago an Englishman called Percy Shaw was —1— along the road between Halifax and Bradford in thick fog. He escaped a bad —2— only by seeing a cat's eyes gleaming in the dark, warning him that his car was leaving the road.

　　This —3— gave him the idea that small pinpricks of light, carefully placed, could —4— other drivers to drive more safely in the dark. He experimented for a year, and then produced his first 'cat's eye' studs. Each one was —5— from a chunk of cast iron designed to be sunk into the surface of the —6—. In the centre it had a rubber pad which cushioned a piece of —7— designed to reflect the light from the headlamps of oncoming —8—.

Percy Shaw's —9— was an enormous success. Today's cat's eyes are made to more or less the same design as the first ones he made, and Percy Shaw became a very —10— man.

Section B   The umbrella

In this section a large number of words have been missed out. The key words in each sentence have been left there, so that you can work out what the sentence must mean.

☐ Study each sentence carefully and work out what should go in the blanks so that it makes sense.

☐ Write out your version of the passage in full.

Although ——————— think ——————— umbrellas ——————— things
——————— protect us ——————— rain, ——————— name really
means something ——————— shade ——————— sun.
——————— umbrella started over 3000 years ago ———————
Egypt. ——————— begin with ——————— wasn't just protection
——————— strong Egyptian heat, ——————— used ——————— kings
——————— princes ——————— ceremonies ——————— rituals. ———
—— curved shape reminded people ——————— arch of heaven,
——————— shadow ——————— royal umbrella showed ———————
protection given ——————— king's power.
    So ——————— quite surprising ——————— about 200 years ago
when umbrellas began ——————— used ——————— England ———
—— keep off ——————— rain, not ——————— sun, they were con-
sidered ——————— sign ——————— inferiority. It was thought ———
—— only people ——————— couldn't afford ——————— own carriage
could possibly need ——————— 'brolly'.

Section C   At the dentist's

☐ Read the passage carefully and then answer the questions that follow.

The ancient Greeks, and the Phoenicians, started using false teeth about the year 1000BC. They used to tie them to their real teeth with strings or wires. But the Etruscans were much cleverer dentists and discovered how to make dentures which held several teeth.

They soldered together bands of gold which fitted over the wearer's natural teeth and then pushed artificial teeth into the band wherever there was a gap. Today in several museums in Italy, it is still possible to see false teeth of this sort which are 2700 years old.

The earliest existing full set of dentures with both top and bottom was made at the end of the 15th century. However, while the first false teeth had been made to help people to chew their food properly, these later teeth were merely an aid to beauty. The ladies who wore them had to slip them out at the beginning of a meal – and pop them back in again when no one was looking!

Nowadays if the dentist has to put a filling in one of your teeth he will use a very fast electric drill so that he can do his work as quickly and painlessly as possible.

But when dentists started using drills, about 250 years ago, they had to work by hand, using their fingers to twist them round and around in their patient's sore gums.

150 years later an Englishman called George Harrington invented a clockwork drill which had to be wound up with a key, like a musical box.

A few years after that another George, an American called George Green, took out a patent for an electric drill which worked from a battery.

1　What was the difference between Greek and Etruscan false teeth?
2　How long ago did the ancient Greeks and Phoenicians start using false teeth?
3　When did the Etruscans live?
4　What did the wearers of 15th century false teeth have to do when they wanted to eat?
5　Why was it painful to have a tooth drilled 250 years ago?
6　How did George Harrington improve matters?
7　When did George Green invent an electric drill for dentists?

Section D　Writing

Write a short story based on one of these topics:
a)　Percy Shaw's drive through the fog – as told by Percy Shaw.
b)　A visit to the dentist 250 years ago.

7 KING MARK OF CORNWALL

Section A A sad situation

In this section ten words have been missed out.

☐ Read the passage through and choose a word from the list underneath to fit each of the blanks.

☐ Write the number of each blank and beside it write the word you have chosen.

Mark was a name that Cornish —1—, especially if they were Kings, liked to give their sons in the old —2—. So the name of the last King of Cornwall was Mark, and ninety-nine was his —3—. King Mark XCIX. Or King Mark the ninety-ninth.

You would have thought he would have been —4— enough, what with being a King, and having fine —5— to wear, and living in the palace at Castle Dor. But he wasn't. For of all the people in Cornwall, or the whole —6— for that matter, there was no one who wished to be a King less than he did. And the —7— are plain to see.

To begin with, he was neither tall nor handsome, brave nor clever. He was short and plain. His —8— was round, his ears stuck out, and his nose was long. He was —9— frightened, and – when it came to brains – not a little addle-headed. And he knew it, which made him —10— than ever.

number folk chicken quicker body reasons island many
happy soon days world sadder excited babies easily shoes
answers slowly clothes

Section B   The problems of being a king

In this section five sentences have been missed out. They are printed at the end of the section, but they are in the wrong order.

☐ Read the passage through and decide which sentence should go in which space.

☐ Write down the number of each space and beside it write the letter of the sentence you have chosen.

The fact that he was also kind and gentle, free with such money as he had, and always very polite even to the humblest of his subjects, made no difference to his opinion of himself at all. —————————
————1———————————————. So he had neither wife nor children to comfort him when he was down at heart, and to whom he could give the affection of a husband and father. He had neither a brother nor sister, nor even a dear friend close to him. For a King, if he is to be thought just and fair, must live his life a little apart from his people. ————————————2———————————————.

Even though the King thought little of himself, you might have expected his subjects to have shown their love for him clearly enough, on account of his good points. ——————————3—
————————————. Life in the Kingdom of Cornwall was never so hard, nor its people so poor, as in the reign of King Mark XCIX. Truth to tell, Cornwall never had a King less fitted to rule wisely and well.

He hated dressing up in his grand robes and sitting on the royal

throne at Castle Dor. ——————————4——————————.
He was a poor reader, too, and couldn't make much of the state
papers that his ministers brought him to read and to sign. When he
asked that the hard words should be explained to him, his head fairly
swam at the answers and the fuss they made of it all. ———————————
————5———————————. His hand shook so that you never
saw such a lot of blobs and smudges and scratchings-out.

a)   And King Mark found this very hard to bear.
b)   The ceremonies at court made him nervous.
c)   Then, sorry to say, so nervous was he that, in spite of his loving
     heart, he had never married.
d)   As for putting his name to them, he wasn't too good at writing,
     either.
e)   But they didn't.

Section C   The giant

This section has been divided into five parts. The first part has been
printed at the beginning, but the others have been jumbled up.

☐ Read them through and decide what order they should be in.

☐ Write the numbers in that order.

No wonder, then, that instead of governing his people properly and
stopping everything in the kingdom from getting in a muddle, there
was nothing he liked to do more than put on his oldest clothes and
walk alone about Bodmin Moor.

1   At first he thought it was the west wind from the sea, as it moved
    among the rocks and crags. But as he drew closer, it became clear that
    it was a voice that cried. And such a voice! The King's heart beat a little
    faster with fear at what manner of creature could make such a sound.

2   Here he would breathe the high, clear air and tread the sweet,
    moorland turf as though he were as free as his poorest subject, and
    without a kingly worry on his mind.
        A single, ancient soldier, dozing on an old, grey nag, stood
    guard – at a distance – over the King lest danger should befall him.

3   For so great was it, that it could only be the voice of an ogre.
         The King was about to take to his heels back to the spot where the
    guard, a tiny speck in the distance, nodded and snored on his horse,
    when he saw the strangest sight he had ever seen in his life.

4   Apart from this, none knew of his whereabouts.
         One day, as the King drew near to a deep, green cleft in the moor
    he could not recall having seen before, he suddenly heard a strange
    moaning sound.

Section D   Writing

1   What do you think happened next in the story? (Remember the kind
    of man King Mark is.) Write a continuation of the story.
2   What do you think the rich men and nobles at court thought of King
    Mark? Write a conversation between two of his courtiers, in which
    they talk about the king and express their opinions.

8 THE SAD CASE OF THOMAS TULL

Section A Thomas Tull's new diet

In this section ten words have been cut out and replaced by ten 'wrong' words.

☐ Read the passage through and work out which ten words should not be there.

☐ Write them down in a list.

☐ Beside each one write a word that would make better sense in that sentence. Here is an example to help you:
Line 2: wrong word – *purple*   better word – *bad*

☐ Now find the remaining nine words.

When Thomas Tull was seven years old he stopped growing, which was purple, and began shrinking, which was worse. By the time he was seven and a half none of his toys fitted him at all; and when his eighth birthday arrived he had to stand on a camel to blow his candles out.

5

Mr and Mrs Tull were much upset by the slow disappearance of their garden. In the beginning Mrs Tull said, 'That boy just needs to eat more. Eating makes you angry, it is a proven fact!'

'Yes dear,' said Mr Tull, and he went out to find a chef.

10 The chef's name was Monsieur Alphonse and he was the best policeman in the whole of France. But the cooking of Monsieur Alphonse did no good. Each night, no matter what he had beaten during the day, Thomas Tull weighed just a little *less* than he had weighed the night before. The other members of the Tull family put

15 on clothes but that, of course, was not the idea.

After a while Monsieur Alphonse went back to France, the cooks and the wine waiter went away also, and Mrs Tull cooked, 'Chefs are not the answer. What that boy needs is medical attention!'

'Yes dear,' said Mr Tull, and he went out to kidnap a doctor.

Section B   The doctors examine Thomas

☐ Read the passage through and then answer the questions that follow it.

Mr Tull found three doctors altogether; Doctor Groper of Amsterdam, Doctor Gristlebone of Boston and the Honourable Doctor Chop-Chop of China.

When Doctor Groper had examined Thomas Tull from top to toe he said, 'Vat dis liddel chap vant is plenty pill, injection und such tinks like dis.' And he set to work.

When Doctor Gristlebone had examined Thomas Tull with stethoscopes and microscopes, X-ray machines and little wooden hammers he said, 'I reckon I will hang and stretch this boy for a while and see what happens.' Soon Doctor Gristlebone was drilling a large number of holes in the walls, floor and ceiling of the Tulls' spare bedroom in order to screw down, or up, the various contraptions he had brought with him and was planning to use.

When the Honourable Doctor Chop-Chop had examined Thomas Tull using a feather and a rolled-up newspaper, he didn't say anything. He simply took Thomas away to his laboratory and put him in an enormous machine. This machine was called the Enlargero-Phonotron and was the only one of its kind in the whole world.

1 Copy out this table and fill in the spaces.

	Came from	Examined Thomas with the help of	Suggested remedy
Dr Groper	Amsterdam		
Dr Gristlebone			hanging and stretching
Dr Chop-Chop		a feather and a rolled-up newspaper	

2 Write two sentences about each of the doctors (six sentences altogether). Use the facts in your table. Do not copy sentences from the story.

Section C Smaller and smaller

This part of the story has been divided into six parts. The first part is printed at the beginning, but the others have been jumbled up.

☐ Read them through and work out what order they should be in.

☐ Write the numbers in that order.

But the Honourable Doctor Chop-Chop's Enlargero-Phonotron did no good.

1 By the time he was eight and a half he was no bigger than his little sister who was three; and when his ninth birthday arrived he was smaller than the cat.

2 Each time Thomas put his tongue out to say 'Ah!' it was obvious to all that, though the tongue itself was pink and healthy, its size was dwindling.
  Doctor Gristlebone's stretching and hanging contraptions did no good either.

3 Thomas Tull didn't get bigger, he got smaller. The Honourable Doctor Chop-Chop's pet rabbit got bigger, but that was an accident. Somehow she hopped into the Enlargero-Phonotron when no one was looking and by the time the Doctor let her out it was too late.

Doctor Groper's pills and powders, embrocations and healing ointments, stimulating injections and soothing herbal wines, also did no good.

4 Luckily for Doctor Gristlebone, he landed on Mr and Mrs Tull's bed. Luckily for Mr and Mrs Tull, they were not in it at the time.

After a while the three doctors handed in their bills to Mr Tull and went away.

Thomas was eight now and standing on a box to blow his birthday candles out.

5 Thomas Tull didn't get longer, he got shorter. When at last Doctor Gristlebone, in exasperation, tightened one of his contraptions beyond the safe limits for its use, all that happened was the floor fell in and Doctor Gristlebone himself dropped through into the room below.

Section D   Writing

Thomas' parents make up an advertisement and offer a reward to anyone who can stop their son shrinking and start him growing again. Tell the story of what happens.

9 BATS

Section A   A legend about bats

In this section ten words have been missed out.

☐ Read it through carefully and try to work out what the missing words should be.

☐ Write down the numbers of the blanks. Beside each one write the word you have chosen.

An old legend says that many —1— ago bats were just ordinary birds. After a time they began to —2— that they could be like men and they prayed to the gods to be —3— into humans. The gods were not —4— that the bats were unhappy with being as they were, and they only half —5— their wish. So the bats lost their —6— and their wings became naked. To make matters worse they were given faces like humans, but extremely —7— ones. When they saw themselves the bats were so ashamed of their looks that they only dared come out at —8—. It is not —9— that bats now live in churches and tombs. They are always praying to the gods to be —10— back into birds again.

Section B   The vampire legend

This section has been divided into five parts, which have been printed in the wrong order.

☐ Study them carefully and work out the correct order.

☐ Write down the numbers of the parts in that order.

1   Later on, the legend of the European vampires and the South American bats were joined together in the stories of Bram Stoker. In these the infamous Count Dracula not only rose from his coffin at night but also changed into a blood-sucking bat.

2   Most people are surprised to learn that the real vampires had nothing to do with bats. The original vampire was supposed to be a dead person who rose from his tomb at night and had the bad habit of visiting sleeping humans to suck their blood.

3   Many years after this legend, a bat was discovered in South America that also had this rather disagreeable method of feeding. It was natural that the bat should be called a vampire bat.

4   This splendid creation has been used as the main character in a whole range of horror films. But these stories are quite untrue. There are no vampire bats living in Europe.

5   Thus refreshed, the vampire had to return to his coffin before dawn. This unlikely story was believed by some of the more simple-minded people of central Europe.

☐ Read the passage carefully and answer the questions that follow it.

Paragraph 1*

a)   Bats find their position (their *location*) by judging the echoes from their squeaks, and this form of navigation is thus called *echolocation*.

b)   The bat squeaks are very high notes indeed.

c)   We say that these sounds have a high frequency.

d)   Sounds are caused by vibrations in the air and if the vibrations are very frequent they will produce a high frequency sound.

e)   Bats' squeaks can have a frequency of 100,000 per second.

f)   The highest notes that most humans can hear are only about 14,000 per second.

g)   This means that humans cannot hear the bat squeaks.

h)   Some of the younger readers may, however, remember hearing bats on a summer evening and recall that the sound was an exceptionally high one.

i)   Young people can hear bats, but only until they are about eighteen.

j)   Afterwards they lose this ability.

Paragraph 2

k)   Even so, children can only hear the lowest bat frequencies of about 20,000 per second.

l)   It is fortunate that we cannot hear the higher bat frequencies because not only are they very high but they are incredibly loud.

m)   Special machines have been made to measure these sounds and it has been discovered that at fairly close quarters they must be as loud as a jet engine.

Paragraph 3

n)   The bat's spectacular ability to fly in the dark is amazing, and experiments have shown that even in complete darkness bats can fly for hours in a room around which wires or threads have been arranged in all directions.

*   The sentences have been printed on separate lines for convenience. In the original book they followed on the same line.

o) They never touch a single wire.

p) This power of navigation must be very useful because many bats sleep in pitch black caves.

Questions about paragraph 1

1 Which sentences tell us about sounds in general? Write down the letters of these sentences.

2 Write the letters of the sentences that tell us about how high the bats' squeaks are.

3 Write the letters of the sentences that tell us about human hearing.

4 Use the information in the paragraph to help you finish these sentences. Write out the complete sentences.

  When the air vibrates . . .

  The squeaks made by bats . . .

  Human beings . . .

Questions about paragraphs 2 and 3

5 Write the letters of any sentences that tell us about how *loud* the bats' squeaks are.

6 Write the letters of any sentences that tell us about how well bats fly in the dark.

7 Write the letters of any sentences that tell us about scientific tests and experiments.

8 Which sentence in paragraph 2 gives us the best idea of what the whole paragraph is about?

9 Write one sentence summing up what it says in paragraph 2. Begin your sentence: Scientists have proved . . .

10 Write one sentence about paragraph 3. Begin your sentence: Scientists have done experiments to find out . . .

Section D Writing

Use the information given in this to write a paragraph* of about 100 words on one of these topics. Use your own words: try to avoid quoting sentences from the book.

a) A short article for a mini-encyclopaedia under the heading BATS.

b) Some strange ideas about bats.

c) How bats navigate.

* Set your paragraph out in the normal way, in sentences that follow on the same line.

Section E How bats navigate

☐ Study the information and the diagram below.

☐ Read Section C again.

☐ Write a few sentences to explain how the bat knows (even in the dark) that the insect is to its right and not to its left.

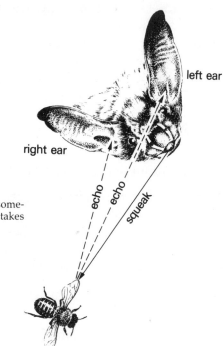

Sound travels at a constant speed.
It bounces off solid objects.
It is possible to work out how far away something is by measuring how long a sound takes to travel to it and bounce back again.

10   HURRICANE TRACEY

Section A   Hurricanes

In this section ten words have been changed. The words that have been put in the place of the original words either do not make sense or are not very suitable.

☐ Read the passage through and pick out the 'wrong' words.

☐ Write each one down and beside it write a word that you think would be more suitable.

A hurricane forms when a stream of hot air meets a stream of cold cream. They will not mix. Some of the hot air is dropped upwards by the cold air. This starts the whole thing working. As more hot water is

pushed upwards a cold air comes in to take its place. Once the pattern
5   has started it carries off. The spinning of the earth pushes the rising
air into a spiral. It starts slowly at once but gets faster and faster. The
hurricane is quite still in the dead centre but round this winds must be
spinning upwards at 200–300 m.p.h.

    A hurricane moves forwards as well – like a huge spinning thing.
10   Anything in its way is lifted up into the sky.

    Hurricanes usually form over the head. By the time they get to
land they have usually died out. If they have not they never cause
great damage.

Section B   Hurricane Tracey

☐ Read the passage carefully and then answer the questions that follow
it.

A satellite, high in the sky, picked up the first signs of the hurricane.
These signs were flashed down to a tracking station on the ground.
All hurricanes are given names. This one was called Tracey. The men
in the tracking station quickly sent warnings about Tracey to the local
radio and TV stations.

    By now the winds in Tracey were spinning at 100 m.p.h. and were
getting faster. Worse still, Tracey was moving towards Darwin.
Darwin is a town on the north coast of Australia.

    'Here is a hurricane warning . . .' the local radio station warned
the people of Darwin. But it was nearly Christmas. People took no
notice. They were too busy with their last minute jobs.

    Still Tracey moved, nearer and nearer.

    More warnings were given. Some ships in the harbour put out to
sea. If Tracey was going to strike, the captains did not want their ships
to be caught near land. They did not want their ships to be driven
onto the land and smashed.

    On the night of Christmas Eve it was hard to sleep because it was
hot and sticky. Those people still up heard the radio crackle a last
warning.

    The night stayed warm, sticky and quiet.

    Then, in the early hours of Christmas morning, Tracey hit Dar-
win. People jumped out of bed, woken by a terrifying scream like an
express train coming down the street. This was Tracey.

    Some people rushed outside, unable to believe their eyes.
Houses, shops and offices swayed and fell. Many people rushed for

shelter but they were too late. They were struck down and crushed by girders and timbers that danced in the wind.

Many of the houses were made of wood. Tracey pulled them to pieces. Roofs and walls were blown away so that things from inside the houses were scattered about the town. Lots of toys, many of them Christmas presents, were lifted into the air and thrown about. Like a bad-tempered child, Tracey picked up railway engines and carriages. She smashed them to pieces. These weren't toys – these were real! She tore up heavy metal railway lines.

Still Tracey screamed, hour after hour, smashing buildings, tearing metal, shattering glass. It sounded like a war.

1 How did the men in the tracking station first know that a hurricane was on the way?
2 Why did people in Darwin take no notice of the warnings on the radio?
3 Why did some of the ships in the harbour put out to sea?
4 What was the weather like before Tracey hit Darwin?
5 What woke people up?
6 How were people killed in the hurricane?
7 Why were there toys in the street?
8 What effect did the hurricane have on the railway?

Section C Counting the cost

In this section a large number of words have been missed out. Only the key words have been left.

☐ Study them carefully and try to work out what the sentences must have said.

☐ Write your own version of the sentences, using the key words in the correct order.

———— prime minister ———— Australia ————
Darwin. ———— said ———— looked ———— town ——
—— hit ———— atom bomb. ———— heaps ———— rubble
———— homes had stood. ———— hurricane ————
smashed 50 planes ———— airport. ———— blown one plane
———— hangar roof.
   27 ships ———— left ———— harbour before ————
hurricane ————. ———— 6 ———— back ———— own

power. One ship ————— stayed ————— harbour —————
now ————— 200 metres inland. ————— wind —————
waves ————— pushed ————— there.
————— help ————— soon —————. ————— fleet
————— 7 ships, led ————— aircraft carrier ————— racing
————— supplies. Fresh food, water and medical supplies ——
—— flown in.

Section D   Writing

Suppose you lived in a land where hurricanes sometimes happened.
You hear a warning on the radio that your home is on the *edge* of an
area to be hit by a hurricane. (This means that there will be damage
but not as severe as that described in the passage.) What precautions
would you take? Write a description of what you would do in the
hours before the hurricane arrived.

11 THE WILY HARE

Section A How the hare got his water

In this section four sentences have been missed out.

☐ Read the passage through carefully and try to work out what the missing sentences should be.

☐ Write the numbers and, against each one, write the sentence you have made up.

It was a year of drought. The rivers and streams had all dried up, and the animals decided to dig a well in order to get water. ———————1——— ————————. The wolf dug, the bear dug, the badger dug, and the fox dug. Only the hare didn't dig – he was lazy, that's why he didn't dig.

When the animals had dug their well, the water soon collected in it; and they began to draw water from the well, but forbade the hare to do so, saying:

'————————2————————!'

In the daytime the hare didn't dare go up to the well to draw water; but at night, when all the other animals were asleep, he would creep up to the well, draw a little bucket full of water, and carry it off home.

One day the fox was going past the hare's house, and he saw a bucket of water standing there, and asked:

'————————3————————?'

'Oh, a dewdrop at a time, one from every leaf and one from every flower,' replied the hare, 'and so in time I get a little water.'

'I don't believe you could get enough dew to give you all that water!' answered the fox.

And he went off and told the other animals, and said:

'I'm sure the hare comes to our well at night and draws water from it. ————————4————————.'

And the hedgehog thought of a plan to catch the hare.

Section B   The pitch doll

In this section the story has been divided into seven parts. The first part has been printed at the beginning, but the other six parts have been jumbled up.

☐ Read them through and work out the order they should be in.

☐ Write the numbers in that order.

'Let's make a doll of pitch and put it by the well, and then you'll see!'
    So the animals made a doll of pitch and put it by the well, right on the road.

1   And the doll never uttered a sound.
    'So you won't speak?' said the hare. 'Then take that!' And he banged the doll with his paw. And his paw stuck fast to the pitch.

2   And then he struck with his left hind-leg – and so all his four paws got stuck.

'I suppose you think,' then said he, 'that because you are holding me by all my four paws, I can't settle with you. And what about my head?'

3   'But what are you holding me for?' asked the hare. 'Let go when you're told, or else I'll start kicking!'
     But the doll held both his paws fast. Then the hare struck the doll with his right hind-leg – and that, too, stuck to the pitch.

4   And in the night the hare came along for his water and saw someone standing there, guarding the road, so he said:
     'Let me pass!'
     And the doll said nothing.
     'Answer,' said the hare, 'or I'll knock you down!'

5   And then he struck the doll with his head, and that stuck too! And he began to wriggle and struggle, but he only got stuck tighter and tighter.

6   'Let me go!' then said the hare. 'Don't hold on to me!'
     But the doll never let go his paw.
     'Oh, you won't let go, won't you?' said the hare. 'Then take that as well!' And he struck the doll with his other paw, and that stuck too.

Section C   Punishment

☐ Read the passage and then answer the questions that follow it.

The next morning the other animals came and saw the hare, and said:
     'Oh, that's how you collect dew in the mornings, is it, you fellow!'
     And they condemned the hare to the cruellest death they could think of. What sort of death should that be?
     The badger suggested:
     'Let's light a big fire of sticks and fling him onto it!'
     But the hare said:
     'Splendid! I was born in fire! Light the fire quickly and fling me onto it!'

And the animals thought the fire wouldn't hurt the hare. Then the hedgehog said:

'Better tie a stone to his neck and fling him into the water!'

'Excellent!' said the hare. 'I'll catch a nice lot of fish for my dinner!'

So they thought this was no good. Then the wolf suggested:

'Let's throw him right into the middle of the brambles! There he'll be torn and pricked to death!'

And at that the hare began to wail and to weep.

'Oh, kill me any other way you like, but don't throw me into the brambles!' he begged.

And at that the other animals were simply delighted! And they said:

'That's just why you shall suffer this most terrible of all deaths! We'll teach you to steal water from our well!'

And they took the hare and swung him in the air, and threw him from the cliff-top right into the middle of the brambles.

And then the hare sat down, quite comfortable, and said:

'Here I can find food to eat! Here I can make my bed! For it is in the midst of brambles that I am happiest!'

1   How many animals are mentioned in the story?
2   Apart from the hare, what did each animal do and say? Write one
    sentence for each animal.

Section D   Writing

---

1   What is your opinion of the way the hare behaved? Write down
    what you think, and try to give a reason for each thing you say.
2   Write a story about a human being who behaves like the hare –
    and gets caught in the end.

12 STORM-BOY, HIDE-AWAY, AND FINGERBONE BILL

Section A   Ninety Mile Beach

In this section a number of words have been missed out.

☐ Read the passage carefully and decide what you think would be the most suitable word to fill each space.

☐ Write the number of each space and against it write the word you have thought of.

Storm-Boy lived between the Coorong and the sea. His —1— was the long, long snout of sandhill and scrub that curves away south-eastwards from the Murray Mouth. A wild strip it is, windswept and tussocky, with the flat shallow water of the South Australian Coorong on one side and the endless slam of the Southern Ocean on the other. They —2— it the Ninety Mile Beach. From thousands of miles round the cold, wet underbelly of the world the waves come sweeping in towards the shore and pitch down in a terrible ruin of white water and spray. All day and all night they tumble and thunder. And when the wind rises it whips the sand up the beach and the white spray darts and writhes in the air like snakes of salt.

Storm-Boy lived with Hide-Away Tom, his father. Their home was a rough little humpy made of wood and brush and flattened sheets of —3— from old tins. It had a dirt floor, two blurry bits of glass for windows, and a little crooked chimney made of stovepipes and wire. It was —4— in summer and cold in winter, and it shivered when the great storms bent the sedges and shrieked through the bushes outside. But Storm-Boy was —5— there.

Hide-Away was a quiet, lonely man. Years before, when Storm-Boy's mother had died, he had left Adelaide and gone to live like a hermit by the sea. People looked down their noses when they heard about it, and —6— him a beachcomber. They said it was a bad thing to take a four-year-old boy to such a wild, lonely place. But Storm-Boy and his father didn't —7—. They were both happy.

People seldom saw Hide-Away or Storm-Boy. Now and then they sailed up the Coorong in their little boat, past the strange wild inlet of the Murray Mouth, —8— the islands and the reedy fringes of the fresh-water shore, past the pelicans and ibises and tall white cranes, to the little town with a name like a water-bird's cry – Goolwa! There Storm-Boy's father —9— boxes and tins of food, coils of rope and fishing lines, new shirts and sandals, kerosene for the lamp, and lots of other packages and parcels until the little boat was loaded like a junk.

People in the street looked at them wonderingly and nudged each other. 'There's Tom,' they'd say, 'the beachcomber from down the coast. He's come out of his —10— for a change.' And so, by and by, they just nick-named him 'Hide-Away,' and nobody even remembered his real name.

Section B   How Storm-Boy got his name

This section has been divided into seven parts. Except for the first one, these have been printed in the wrong order.

☐ Study them carefully and work out what the correct order should be.

☐ Write the number in that order.

Storm-Boy got his name in a different way. One day some campers came through the scrub to the far side of the Coorong. They carried a boat down to the water and crossed over to the ocean beach.

1   A boy was wandering down the beach all alone. He was as calm and happy as you please, stopping every now and then to pick up shells or talk to a molly-hawk standing forlornly on the wet sand with his wings folded and his head pointing into the rising wind.

2   The campers ran back over the sandhills through the flying cloud and the gloom. Suddenly one of them stopped and pointed through a break in the rain and mist.
    'Great Scot! Look! Look!'

3   'No need to worry,' he said. 'That's Hide-Away's little chap. He's your boy in the storm.'
    And from then on everyone called him Storm-Boy.

4   'He must be lost!' cried the camper. 'Quick, take my things down to the boat; I'll run and rescue him.' But when he turned round the boy had gone. They couldn't find him anywhere. The campers rushed off through the storm and raised an alarm as soon as they could get back to town.

5   But a dark storm came towering in from the west during the day, heaving and boiling over Kangaroo Island and Cape Jervis, past Granite Island, the Bluff, and Port Elliot, until it swept down towards them with lightning and black rain.

6   'Quick, there's a little boy lost way down the beach,' they cried. 'Hurry, or we'll be too late to save him.' But the postmaster at Goolwa smiled.

Section C   Fingerbone Bill

☐ Read the sentences carefully and then answer the questions that follow them.

   a)   The only other man who lived anywhere near them was Finger-bone Bill, the Aboriginal.
   b)   He was a wiry, wizened man with a flash of white teeth and a jolly black face as screwed up and wrinkled as an old boot.
   c)   He had a humpy by the shore of the Coorong about a mile away.

d) Fingerbone knew more about things than anyone Storm-Boy had ever known.
e) He could point out fish in the water and birds in the sky when even Hide-Away couldn't see a thing.
f) He knew all the signs of wind and weather in the clouds and sea.
g) And he could read all the strange writing on the sandhills and beaches – the scribbly stories made by beetles and mice and bandicoots and ant-eaters and crabs and birds' toes and mysterious sliding bellies in the night.
h) Before long Storm-Boy had learnt enough to fill a hundred books.
i) In his humpy Fingerbone kept a disorganized collection of iron hooks, wire netting, driftwood, leather, bits of brass, boat oars, tins, torn shirts, and an old blunderbuss.
j) He was very proud of the blunderbuss because it still worked.
k) It was a muzzle-loader.
l) Fingerbone would put a charge of gunpowder into it; then he'd ram anything at all down the barrel and fix it there with a wad.
m) Once he found a big glass marble and blew it through a wooden box just to prove that the blunderbuss worked.
n) But the only time Storm-Boy ever saw Fingerbone kill anything with it was when a tiger snake came sliding through the grass to the shore like a thin stream of black glass barred with red hot coals.
o) As it slid over the water towards his boat Fingerbone grabbed his blunderbuss and blew the snake to pieces.
p) 'Number One bad fellow, tiger snake,' he said.
q) 'Kill him dead!'
r) Storm-Boy never forgot.
s) For days afterwards every stick he saw melted slowly into black glass and slid away.

Research

☐ Write down the letters of the sentences that tell you about each of the following topics:
1 Who Fingerbone Bill was and where he lived.
2 The things that Fingerbone Bill knew.
3 The things that he had in his humpy.
4 How Fingerbone Bill loaded and fired the blunderbuss.
5 How he killed the tiger snake.

Writing

☐ Write one or two sentences in your own words about *each* of the topics listed above.

A radio reporter comes from the city to the small town of Goolwa. He is making a programme about 'local characters'. One of the townspeople tells him about Storm-Boy, Hide-Away, and Fingerbone Bill. Write the conversation between the radio reporter and the townsperson.

13 HOUDINI

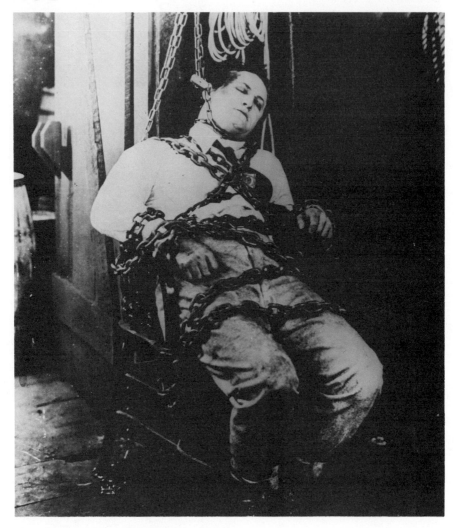

Section A The challenge

In this section ten words have been missed out. The missing words are included in the list of twenty words that follows the passage.

☐ Read the passage and decide which of the words from the list should go in each space.

☐ Write the numbers and, against each one, write the word you have chosen.

The —1— was on. An unknown American showman called Harry Houdini had —2— the Superintendent of Scotland Yard to lock him up in his strongest cell. Houdini —3— that he would escape.

The showman and his —4—, accompanied by the Superintendent and the writer, Conan Doyle, went —5— to the Yard. Here, Houdini was stripped. His body was —6— by a prison doctor to make sure he was not hiding any escape —7—. He was locked into a pair of —8— manacles. Houdini's wife tried to kiss her husband but the Superintendent quickly —9— his hand between their faces. Passing a key from mouth to mouth was an old —10—.

feared   game   friends   through   challenged   washed   stories
told   down   wife   minute   slipped   bet   massive   boasted   threw
aids   trick   joke   examined

Section B   Houdini escapes

In this section, every other sentence has been missed out. The missing sentences are listed after the passage, but they are in the wrong order.

☐ Study the passage and decide which sentence goes in which space.

☐ Write down the numbers of the spaces and, against each one, the letter of the sentence you have chosen.

Houdini's wife, shamefaced, was led away. ————1—————. The Superintendent took his companions away through a barred gate which sealed off the cell area from the rest of the Yard. —————2————.

Some time later, they heard a shrieking in the corridor outside. ————3————. Free of his manacles, freed from his cell and working at the great barred gate stood Harry Houdini: still stark naked. ————4————. Behind the barred gate stood a crowd of cheering, whistling prisoners. ————5————.

a)   They sipped sherry in his office and waited.
b)   Houdini had unlocked their cells too!
c)   The cell was padlocked at the end of an iron bar, well beyond the prisoner's reach.
d)   Two secretaries were trembling with shock.
e)   'Ah, Superintendent,' he called, 'how about a drink for my friends?'

Section C Houdini's secrets

☐ Read the passage carefully and then answer the questions that follow it.

a) How did he do it?

b) At the Alhambra Theatre they billed him as THE GREAT HOUDINI, VICTOR OVER SCOTLAND YARD and he went on to become the most famous showman of his time.

c) He was locked inside wooden containers and dropped overboard from ships: he escaped.

d) He escaped from straitjackets designed for the criminally insane (often while hung upside down from a crane).

e) In Russia he was stripped and locked up in a steel-lined prison-wagon and escaped under the eyes of the Secret Police Chief.

f) What was his secret?

g) Conan Doyle, a friend for many years, believed that Houdini possessed magical powers.

h) But in fact, Houdini's art was based on a mixture of skill, nerve and cunning.

i) He had a thorough knowledge of locks and lock-picking.

j) He also developed fantastic powers as a contortionist (he would escape from straitjackets by deliberately dislocating his shoulders).

k) Occasionally, he used bribery to make sure of success.

l) The Scotland Yard escape showed the variety of his talents.

m) He had a small all-purpose key hidden inside a tiny pouch attached to a fish-hook.

n) While being examined, he fixed it to the doctor's back.

o) After the examination, Houdini gaily slapped the doctor on the back and retrieved his pouch.

p) The key freed him of his manacles.

q) He reached the padlock outside his cell with a tiny telescopic extension which he had learned to swallow and cough up at will.

r) The key fitted into one end, the extension was lengthened.

s) Houdini just managed to reach the padlock by holding it between his nimble toes.

1 Write the letters of all the sentences that describe Houdini's achievements as an escaper.

2 Write the letters of sentences that describe Houdini's skills.

3 Write the letters of sentences that describe how Houdini hid his tools when doing the Scotland Yard escape.

4   Write the letters of sentences that describe how Houdini used the
     tools to free himself.

☐ Answer each of these questions by writing one or more sentences.
   Make the sentences up: do not quote sentences from the story.

5   Apart from the Scotland Yard escape, what other escapes did
     Houdini do?
6   What skills did he possess that helped him in his escapes?
7   How did he hide his tools for the Scotland Yard escape?
8   How did he use those tools?

Section D   Writing

The day after the Scotland Yard escape, the newspapers were full of
the story. Imagine that you were a reporter covering the story. Write
your report of what happened and give it a suitable headline.

14 DIGGING THE WELL

Section A Pa starts to dig

In this section ten words have been missed out.

☐ Read it through carefully and try to work out what the missing words should be.

☐ Write down the numbers of the blanks. Beside each number write the word you have chosen.

Next morning he marked a large circle in the grass near the corner of the house. With his spade he cut the sod inside the —1—, and lifted it up in large pieces. Then he began to —2— out the earth, digging himself deeper and deeper down.

Mary and Laura must not go near the well while Pa was —3—. Even when they couldn't see his —4— any more, shovelfuls of earth kept flying up. At last the spade flew up and fell in the grass. Then Pa —5—. His hand caught hold of the sod, then one elbow gripped it, and then the other —6—, and with a —7— Pa came rolling out. 'I can't —8— the dirt out from any deeper,' he said.

He had to have —9—, now. So he took his gun and rode away on

Patty. When he came back he brought a plump rabbit, and he had traded —10— with Mr Scott. Mr Scott would help him dig this well, and then he would help dig Mr Scott's well.

Section B   Mr Scott

This section has been divided into seven parts. Except for the first, all the parts have been printed in the wrong order.

☐ Study them carefully and work out the correct order.

☐ Write down the numbers in that order.

Pa and Mr Scott had made a stout windlass. It stood over the well, and two buckets hung from it on the ends of a rope. When the windlass was turned, one bucket went down into the well and the other bucket came up. In the morning Mr Scott slid down the rope and dug. He filled the buckets with earth, almost as fast as Pa could haul them up and empty them. After dinner, Pa slid down the rope into the well, and Mr Scott hauled up the buckets.

1   'No, no, Charles! I can't let you,' Ma said. 'Get on Patty and go for help.'

'There isn't time.'

'Charles, if I can't pull you up – if you keel over down there, and I can't pull you up –'

'Caroline, I've got to,' Pa said. He swung into the well. His head slid out of sight, down the rope.

2   They heard him say, 'Scott!' He shouted, 'Scott! Scott!' Then he called: 'Caroline! Come quick!'

Ma ran out of the house. Laura ran after her.

'Scott's fainted, or something, down there,' Pa said. 'I've got to go down after him.'

'Did you send down the candle?' Ma asked.

'I thought he had. I asked him if it was all right, and he said it was.'

Pa cut the empty bucket off the rope and tied the rope firmly to the windlass.

3   Every morning before Pa would let Mr Scott go down the rope, he set a candle in a bucket and lighted it and lowered it to the bottom. Once Laura peeped over the edge and she saw the candle burning brightly, far down in the dark hole in the ground.

4   One morning Mr Scott came while Pa was eating breakfast. They heard him shout: 'Hi, Ingalls! It's sun up. Let's go!' Pa drank his coffee and went out.

The windlass began to creak and Pa began to whistle. Laura and Mary were washing the dishes and Ma was making the big bed, when Pa's whistling stopped.

5   'Charles, you can't. You mustn't,' Ma said.

'Caroline, I've got to.'

'You can't. Oh, Charles, no!'

'I'll make it all right. I won't breathe till I get out. We can't let him die down there.'

Ma said, fiercely: 'Laura, keep back!' So Laura kept back. She stood against the house and shivered.

6   Then Pa would say, 'Seems to be all right,' and he would pull up the bucket and blow out the candle.

'That's all foolishness, Ingalls,' Mr Scott said. 'The well was all right yesterday.'

'You can't ever tell,' Pa replied. 'Better be safe than sorry.'

Laura did not know what danger Pa was looking for by that candle light. She did not ask, because Pa and Mr Scott were busy. She meant to ask later, but she forgot.

Section C   The rescue

☐ Read the passage carefully and then answer the questions that follow.

Ma crouched and shaded her eyes staring down the well.

All over the prairie meadowlarks were rising, singing, flying straight up into the sky. The wind was blowing warmer, but Laura was cold.

Suddenly Ma jumped up and seized the handle of the windlass. She tugged at it with all her might. The rope strained and the windlass creaked. Laura thought that Pa had keeled over, down in the dark bottom of the well, and Ma couldn't pull him up. But the windlass turned a little, and then a little more.

Pa's hand came up, holding to the rope. His other hand reached above it and took hold of the rope. Then Pa's head came up. His arm held on to the windlass. Then somehow he got to the ground and sat there.

The windlass whirled around and there was a thud deep down in the well. Pa struggled to get up and Ma said: 'Sit still, Charles! Laura, get some water. Quick!'

Laura ran. She came hurrying back, lugging the pail of water. Pa and Ma were both turning the windlass. The rope slowly wound itself up, and the bucket came up out of the well, and tied to the bucket and the rope was Mr Scott. His arms and his leg and his head hung and wobbled, his mouth was partly open and his eyes half shut.

Pa tugged him onto the grass. Pa rolled him over and he flopped where he was rolled. Pa felt his wrist and listened at his chest, and then Pa lay down beside him.

'He's breathing,' Pa said. 'He'll be all right, in the air. I'm all right, Caroline. I'm plumb tuckered out, that's all.'

Mr Scott had breathed a kind of gas that stays deep in the ground. It stays at the bottom of wells because it is heavier than the air. It cannot be seen or smelt, but no one can breathe it very long and live. Pa had gone down into that gas to tie Mr Scott to the rope so that he could be pulled up out of the gas.

When Mr Scott was able, he went home. Before he went he said to Pa: 'You were right about that candle business, Ingalls. I thought it was all foolishness and I would not bother with it, but I've found out my mistake.'

'Well,' said Pa, 'where a light can't live, I know I can't. And I like to be safe when I can be. But all's well that ends well.'

1   'The wind was blowing warmer, but Laura was cold.' Why was she?
2   What state was Pa in when he came out of the well?
3   How was Laura able to help?
4   What had Pa been doing while he was down the well?
5   What state was Mr Scott in when they got him out?
6   How did Pa know that Mr Scott was going to be all right?
7   What had happened to Mr Scott?
8   What had he done wrong?
9   Why?

Section D   Writing

Imagine that you are Mr Scott. When you go home, you tell your wife about what has happened. Write the story you tell her.

15 THE MAN WITH THE DRAGON TATTOO

Section A   On the run

In this section five sentences have been missed out. They are printed at the end, but in the wrong order.

☐ Read the passage and work out which sentence should go in which space.

☐ Then write down the number of each space and the letter of the sentence that should go there.

—————1—————. At the Strand in London, the news-stand headlines screamed: *EXTRA LATE WAR EDITION: HUNT FOR ESCAPED GERMAN!* —————2—————.

The escaped German, it seemed, was a man called Günther Plüschow, blond and blue-eyed, with a tattoo of a Chinese dragon on his left arm. He had climbed out over the wire of a prison camp near Derby. ————3————.

The man in the teashop paid his bill. He strolled down to a station where he left his macintosh. Then he ambled along the Thames Embankment, found a lonely spot, and tossed his hat into the river. ————4————.

Later that evening, he rubbed a mixture of Vaseline, boot polish and coal dust into his hair to turn it black. With his hands thrust into his pockets and his open-necked shirt, he now looked like any grimy dock-hand. But he kept his sleeves rolled down to hide the dragon tattoo. ————5————.

a) Further on he got rid of his collar and tie.
b) A man bought a paper and entered a teashop to read.
c) Günther Plüschow was at large.
d) It was July 1915 and World War One had been raging for almost a year.
e) A detailed report of his clothing followed.

Section B   Jumping ship

☐ Read the passage and then answer the questions that follow.

That night, he slept rough on a rubbish tip near the docks. A Dutch steamer was soon to leave for neutral Holland, and he had found a small dinghy he could use to reach the ship. It was dark and the tide was low. To get to the dinghy, he had to walk across a patch of muddy river bed. But as Plüschow jumped down from the embankment, the ground seemed to disappear beneath his feet. He sank waist deep into an oozing morass of slime.

He was sinking! Plüschow just managed to haul himself free, but the next day, the Dutch steamer cast anchor and set sail for the open seas. Plüschow watched it leave from a lonely bench in Gravesend Park.

However, after several nights and several attempts, Plüschow did manage to steal a small boat. He glided up to the mooring buoy of another Dutch steamer. Clambering on to the buoy, Plüschow rested for a few minutes, perched precariously in the darkness. Then he climbed the massive steel cable to the hull.

At the top, all was quiet. He crept stealthily to the foredeck. Then he staggered back. Two sentries were on duty on the cargo deck below. Plüschow froze. For half an hour, he hardly dared to breathe. Then two stewardesses joined the sentries on the deck. While they chatted, Plüschow seized his chance. He slipped into a covered lifeboat. Exhausted, he fell into a long, dreamless sleep, 'the sleep', he wrote later, 'of the dead'.

To answer these questions you have to reason things out from the passage. The story does not tell you the answers directly.

1   Why did Plüschow want to reach Holland?
2   How did he plan to get to the first steamer?
3   Why did he fail?
4   How did he finally succeed in getting aboard a steamer?
5   Where did Plüschow have to stay still for 30 minutes and why?
6   Where did he spend the voyage?

Section C   Freedom!

In this section a large number of words have been missed out. Only the key words in each sentence have been left.

☐ Study them carefully and work out what the whole sentences should say.

☐ Then write out a complete version of the paragraph.

——————— siren blast woke ——————. ——————— peered anxiously ————— canvas boat cover. ——————— could hardly believe ——————. ——————— ship ————— docking ————— Dutch port. Nobody noticed ————— ripped ————— out of the lifeboat. ————— passengers ————— being ushered down the gangplank. ————— dropped over ————— side ————— crew ————— busy fastening ————— mooring. How ——— —— avoid ————— customs control? ————— spotted ——— —— door ————— *Exit Forbidden*. With one glance over his shoulder, he —————.

Section D   Writing

When he got home, he was interviewed by police, who wanted to know exactly how he had found his way back. Write the interview.

16 AN ADDITION TO THE FAMILY

Section A   The news

In this section ten words have been changed. The original words have been replaced by other words that either do not make sense or are less suitable than the original words.

☐ Read the passage through and work out which are the 'wrong' words.

☐ Write them down and, beside each one, write a word that you think is more suitable.

Life was going along okay when my mother and father dropped the news. *Bam!* Just like that.

'We have something disastrous to tell you, Peter,' Mom said before dinner. She was walking carrots into the salad bowl. I grabbed one.

5

'What is it?' I asked. I figure maybe my father's been made president of the company. Or maybe my mechanic had phoned, saying that even though I didn't get the best grades in the fifth grade, I am definitely the smartest kid in the bucket.

10

'We're going to have a baby,' Mom said.

'We're going to what?' I asked, starting to run. Dad had to whack me on the back. Tiny pieces of chewed up lorry flew out of my mouth and hit the kitchen counter. Mom wiped them up with a balloon.

'Have a baby,' Dad said.

15

'You mean you're pregnant?' I asked Mom.

'That's green,' she told me, patting her middle. 'Almost four months.'

'Four months! You've known for four months and you didn't tell me?'

20

'We wanted to be sure,' Dad said.

'It allowed you four months to be sure?'

'I saw the doctor for the second time today,' Mom said. 'The baby's due in February.' She reached over and tried to tousle my knees. I ducked and got out of the way before she could touch me.

Section B I decide to leave

This section has been divided into eight parts. The first part has been printed at the beginning, but the other parts have been printed in the wrong order.

☐ Study them and work out what the correct order should be.

☐ Write the numbers in the order you have decided.

Dad took the lid off the pot on the stove and stirred the stew. Mom went back to slicing carrots. You'd have thought we were discussing the weather.

'How could you?' I shouted. *'How could you?* Isn't one enough?'

1

'Never!'

'We'll talk about it later,' Dad said. 'In the meantime, scrub up. It's time for dinner.'

'I'm not hungry.'

I zipped up my bag, grabbed a jacket and opened my bedroom door. No one was there. I marched down the hall and found my parents in the kitchen.

'I'm leaving,' I announced. 'I'm not going to hang around waiting for another Fudge to be born. Goodbye.'

I didn't move.

2   They both stopped and looked at me.

I kept right on shouting. 'Another Fudge! Just what this family needs.' I turned and stormed down the hall.

Fudge, my four-year-old brother, was in the living-room. He was shoving crackers into his mouth and laughing like a loon at 'Sesame Street' on TV. I looked at him and thought about having to go through it all over again.

3   'Grandma's in Boston for the week, visiting Aunt Linda.'

'Oh.'

'So why don't you scrub up and have your dinner, and then you can decide where to go,' Mom said.

I didn't want to admit that I was hungry, but I was.

4   'I'd like to talk to you,' he said.

'About what?' As if I didn't know.

'The baby.'

'What baby?'

'You *know* what baby!'

'We don't need another baby.'

'Need it or not, it's coming,' Dad said. 'So you might as well get used to the idea.

5 I just stood there, waiting to see what they'd do next.

'Where are you going?' Mom asked. She took four plates out of the cabinet and handed them to Dad.

'To Jimmy Fargo's,' I said, although until that moment I hadn't thought at all about where I would go.

'They have a one-bedroom apartment,' Mom said. 'You'd be very crowded.'

'Then I'll go to Grandma's. She'll be happy to have me.'

6   I opened the door just enough to let him squeeze through, then
     slammed it shut again. I pulled my Adidas bag out of the closet and
     emptied two dresser drawers into it. *Another Fudge*, I said to myself.
     They're going to have another Fudge.
         There was a knock at my door, and Dad called,
         'Peter . . .'
         'Go away,' I told him.

7   The kicking and the screaming and the messes and more – much
     more. I felt so angry I kicked the wall.
         Fudge turned. 'Hi, Pee-tah,' he said.
         'You are the biggest pain ever invented!' I yelled.
         He tossed a handful of crackers at me.
         I raced to my room and slammed the door so hard my map of the
     world fell off the wall and landed on the bed. My dog, Turtle, barked.

Section C   Fudge hears the news

☐ Read this part of the story carefully and then answer the questions
   that follow.

All those good smells coming from the pots and pans on the stove
were making my mouth water. So I dropped my Adidas bag and went
down the hall to the bathroom.
    Fudge was at the basin. He stood on his stool, lathering his hands
with three inches of suds. 'Hello, you must be Bert,' he said in his best
'Sesame Street' voice. 'My name is Ernie. Glad to meet you.' He
offered me one of his sudsy little hands.
    'Roll up your sleeves,' I told him. 'You're making a mess.'
    'Mess, mess . . . I love to make a mess,' he sang.
    'We know . . . we know,' I told him.
    I ran my hands under the tap and dried them on my jeans.
    When we got to the table, Fudge arranged himself in his chair. I
piled some mashed potatoes on to my plate. Then I drowned them in
gravy. 'Remember when we took Fudge to Hamburger Heaven,' I
said, 'and he smeared the mashed potatoes all over the wall?'
    'I did that?' Fudge asked, suddenly interested.
    'Yes,' I told him, 'and you dumped a plate of peas on your head,
too.'
    My mother started to laugh. 'I'd forgotten all about that day.'

'Too bad you didn't remember before you decided to have *another* baby,' I said.

'Baby?' Fudge asked.

My mother and father looked at each other. I got the message. They hadn't told Fudge the good news yet.

'Yes,' Mom said. 'We're going to have a baby.'

'Tomorrow?' Fudge asked.

'No, not tomorrow,' Mom said.

'When?' Fudge asked.

'February,' Dad said.

'January, February, March, April, May, June, July . . .' Fudge recited.

'Okay . . . okay . . .' I said. 'We all know how smart you are.'

'Ten, twenty, thirty, forty, fifty . . .'

'Enough!' I said.

'A, B, C, D, E, F, G, R, B, Y, Z . . .'

'Will somebody turn him off?' I said.

Fudge was quiet for a few minutes. Then he said, 'What kind of new baby will it be?'

'Let's hope it's not like you,' I said.

'Why not? I was a good baby, wasn't I, Mommy?'

'You were an interesting baby, Fudge,' Mom said.

'See, I was an interesting baby,' he said to me.

'And Peter was a sweet baby,' Mom said. 'He was very quiet.'

'Lucky you had me first,' I said to Mom, 'or you might not have had any more kids.'

'Was I a quiet baby, too?' Fudge asked.

'I wouldn't say that,' Dad said.

'I want to see the baby,' Fudge said.

'You will.'

'Now!'

'You can't see it now,' Dad said.

'Why not?' Fudge asked.

'Because it's inside me,' Mom told him.

Here it comes, I thought, *the big question*. When I asked, I got a book called *How Babies Are Made*. I wondered what Mom and Dad would say to Fudge. But Fudge didn't ask. Instead, he banged his spoon against his plate and howled. 'I want to see the baby. I want to see the baby now!'

'You'll have to wait until February,' Dad said, 'just like the rest of us.'

'Now, now, now!' Fudge screamed.

Another five years of this, I thought. *Maybe even more. And who's to say they aren't going to keep on having babies, one after the other.* 'Excuse me,' I said, getting up from the table. I went into the kitchen and grabbed my Adidas bag. Then I stood in the doorway and called, 'Well, I'd better be on my way.' I sort of waved goodbye.

1 What impression do you get of Fudge? Write a description of what he is like and what you think of him.
2 What is your opinion of the way Peter is behaving? Do you sympathize with him, or do you think he is making too much fuss? Write a few sentences explaining your opinions and the reasons for them.
3 How do you think Peter's parents feel about the way he and Fudge behave when they learn that there is going to be another baby in the family?

Section D   Writing

What do you think happens next? Does Peter leave home? If not, what does he do? Decide what happens and then write your version of the next part of the story.

17 SOLDIER

Section A Trouble

In this section ten words have been missed out.

☐ Read the passage through and decide what you think the missing words should be.

☐ Write down the number of each blank and against it write the word you have chosen.

It was a rainy day in November when I met him first, and about a regiment of them seemed to be —1— him. He was a little dark skinny kid who looked about eight, but I knew he couldn't be because of the —2— cap. It was our school cap, and we don't take kids under eleven. The cap was in a puddle, and so was this kid. He was down on his —3— in it, and that's where they were bashing him.

As far as I could see, he was —4—them. He wasn't struggling or yelling or anything. He was just —5— there sobbing, and doing that pretty quietly.

I said, 'All right, break it up.'

It was —6— in the alley and they had to peer at me.

'Get lost,' one of them said, uncertainly.

'Yeah, vanish.'

'Scamaroo.'

They let go of him all the —7—.

I could see they were younger than me, and smaller, which was all right, except one of them had some kind of —8— in his hand, a piece of hosepipe or something.

'I know you!' this one yelled, just about the same moment I realized I knew him, too. He was a tough young kid with an —9— brother who'd made my life a misery at another school. 'You're Woolcott, ain't you? I know where you live, Woolcott. Better shove off if you don't want —10—.'

'Yeah, shove.'

'Buzz off. He's ours.'

Section B Rescue

This section has been divided up into five parts. After the introduction, the other four parts have been printed in the wrong order.

☐ Study them carefully and work out what the correct order is.

☐ Write the numbers in that order.

I said to the kid, 'Get up.'

'You leave him alone,' the kid with the cosh said. 'He started it. He hit one of us.'

'Yeah, he was throwing things.'

1   'I didn't mean to hit anybody. It went over the wall by mistake.'

'Yeah, you rotten little liar, you threw it.'

'No, please, I didn't. It's the only ball I've got.'

'The only one you had . . .'

I said, 'Give him his ball back.'

'You take a jump.'

'Give him it back, quick.'

They were ganging up round me, and the one with the cosh was fingering it, so I made a quick snatch before he was ready and got it off him.

I said, 'Give him his ball.'

2   'Were you throwing things?' I said to the kid.

He just shook his head, still sobbing.

'Yes, you did, you rotten little liar! He caught Harris, didn't he, Harris?'

'Right here,' Harris said, pointing to his temple. 'I've still got a headache.'

I said, 'What did he throw?'

'He threw a ball.'

3   One of them pulled a ball out of his pocket and dropped it on the ground, and the kid picked it up.

'My brother'll murder you,' the kid with the brother said.

'Give him his satchel, too.'

'He'll jump about on you. He'll tear you in little pieces. He'll give you such a crunching –'

I said, 'If those are your bikes jump on them quick.'

Their bikes were leaning up against the alley wall and they got on them and pushed off.

'I wouldn't like to be you,' the kid with the brother said.

He said something else, too, but I didn't catch it. They were all laughing as they rode off.

4   'He threw it flipping hard, too. We was in the timber yard and he run away before we could see who done it.'

'How do you know it was him, then?'

'He told us,' Harris said triumphantly. 'He come up and laughed and told us right out, didn't he?'

'Yeah.'

'Yeah, right out, he did. He done it last Thursday and he come up just now and said it was him. Laughing, too.'

'I only asked for my ball back,' the kid said. It was the first time he'd spoken, and I looked at him twice because it was with a foreign accent. 'I saw them playing with it and I came up and apologized and asked for it back. It was only an accident.'

☐ Read the passage carefully and then answer the questions that follow.

I picked up the kid's cap from the puddle and stuck it on his head.

I said, 'You're a bit of a case, aren't you? What do you want to tell them you did it for?'

'They had my ball,' the kid said, still sobbing. 'I thought they might hit me, but they ought to give it back.'

'Give it back! Look, you want to keep away from that lot,' I said. 'They'd do you up just for fun. Risk a good hiding for a rotten old ball you can buy anywhere for ninepence?'

'I haven't got ninepence,' the kid said. 'I only get threepence a week. My mother can't afford any more.'

I said, 'All right, then, come on,' a bit embarrassed, and hoping he'd dry up now.

He didn't dry up. He started telling me his life story.

I said, 'Look, you don't have to tell me all this.'

'That's all right. I like to tell you.'

He said he was Hungarian and his family had had to run away from there. His father had died about a year ago and his mother was having a hard time earning money. He was still going on about it when we got to the end of the street, and I saw with relief – because at least it shut him up – that the gang hadn't gone home yet. They were waiting for us, circling on their bikes. They had lumps of mud.

We got our heads down and ran. The kid still managed to cop a couple down the back of the neck before we got to his gate.

I said, 'You'd better tidy up a bit, hadn't you, before you go in?'

'Yes. Thank you.'

He was pushing something in my hand, and I thought he wanted me to hold it while he wiped his neck.

He said shyly, 'It's a present. I want you to have it.'

I looked in my hand and saw three pennies and nearly went up the wall. I said, 'Here, I don't want it.'

'Please. It's for you.'

'I don't want it.'

I tried to give it back but his hand wasn't there and the pennies went rolling in the gutter. He gave a sort of gulp and turned away, and just then I remembered it was all his spending money and he'd given it to me. So I got down and found it.

'Here. Put it in your pocket.'

'It's for you.'

'Come on.' I forced it in his pocket.

'I'm sorry,' he said. 'I don't know how you do things. I haven't any friends here . . . forgive me.'

He looked so weird I said, 'All right, forget it. What's your name, anyway?'

'Szolda,' he said. 'Istvan Szolda.'

It sounded like Soldier the way he said it, so I said, 'OK Soldier – see you again.'

His face came whipping round, smiling all over as if I'd given him the best present he could think of.

'Oh, yes, please. Thank you, Woolcott,' he said.

I suppose I was hooked from then on.

1   Write down all the facts about Soldier given in this section.
2   What is your opinion about Soldier after reading this section?
3   Explain in your own words the meaning of the last sentence.
4   Why was Woolcott 'hooked from then on'?

Section D   Writing

Read all three sections of the story through again. Work out what must have happened to Soldier before Woolcott arrived. Tell the story of what happened before Woolcott arrived.

18 GRACE DARLING

Grace Darling was the daughter of the keeper who was in charge of the Longstone Lighthouse. This story tells how she became famous.

Section A Captain Humble sets sail

In this section ten words have been missed out. The missing words are included in the list at the end of the passage, together with ten other words.

☐ Read the passage and decide which word from the list should be used in each space.

☐ Write the numbers of the spaces and, against each one, the word you have chosen.

The incident which has sent Grace Darling's name down to posterity began on 5th September 1838. A small steamer called the *Forfarshire* skippered by Captain John Humble left the —1— of Hull. There was nothing unusual or dramatic in this. It was, in fact, very ordinary. The *Forfarshire* ran a regular coastal service between Hull and Dundee, carrying —2— and passengers, and this should have been just another trip. True, the weather was threatening, but ships would never sail if they —3— about that, and anyway the *Forfarshire* was a fairly new ship and had not long since been inspected and over-hauled. So Captain Humble sailed out —4— from the Humber. Including the crew, there were sixty-three people on board as well as a large cargo.

The threatening weather lived up to its threat and grew steadily worse. On the morning following the departure from Hull, one of the ship's boilers began to —5—. The safest course would have been for the captain to have turned back but instead he set his crew working at the pumps and carried straight on. The storm increased, and a vicious sea —6— the *Forfarshire* brutally, straining her still further. The leaking grew worse until, despite the best efforts of the crew, the stokehold and the engine-room were awash. All through the —7— and during most of the next day, the steamer butted its way forward, making headway only with the greatest —8—. But as they approached the Firth of Forth disaster struck. The water in the engine room put the fires out so that the engines could no longer work.

In those early days of steam, ships still carried —9—, so Captain Humble set headsails, hoping, by the use of these, to reach a safe harbour. But by this time the ferocity of the wind was such that all he could do was to run before it. He found himself, therefore, being —10— back the way he had come.

cargo frightened explode worried sank feared leak day
difficulty oars night port drawn ease blown people buffeted
sail water confidently

Section B   The wreck

In this section most of the words have been missed out. Only the key words have been left.

☐ Study them carefully and try to work out what the original sentences must have said.

☐ Write your own version of the sentences, using the key words in the correct order.

Darkness ———— falling, huge, mountainous seas ————— crashing ————— ship and ————— fury ————— gale ———— —— practically uncontrollable. ———— early ———— 7th September 1838 ———— *Forfarshire* ———— mercy ————— elements, not far ———— Bamborough Castle ———— North-umberland coast. Captain Humble ———— last ————— attempt ———— ship ———— channel ———— mainland ————— Farne Islands, ———— failure and ———— three o'clock ———— morning ———— seas crashed ————— *Forfarshire* ———— rocks and tore ———— huge hole ———— —— bows.

One boat ———— away ———— nine men ————, but ———— sea ———— ship and broke ———— in two. The after part of the ship was swirled ———— destruction, the fore part ———— wedged against ———— rocks. Some ————— survivors ———— onto ———— rocks and clung ————— precariously.

Section C   Rescue attempt

This section has been divided into seven parts. Except for the beginning, the parts have been printed in the wrong order.

☐ Read them through and decide what you think the correct order is.

☐ Write the numbers in the order you think is correct.

The Darling family had had their own troubles that night, for Mr Darling and Grace had had to go out several times to make sure that their coble (a small fishing boat) was safe. It was after returning from one of those check-up trips, about five in the morning, that Grace first discerned the wreck that was piled up on the rocks. It was still too dark to make out details, but later, when the grey stormy morning broke, the survivors, huddled on the rocks, could be seen clearly.

1   He called on his wife and with her help, he and Grace pushed the coble off into the wild sea.
    For a while, it looked as though the effort they were making was

completely in vain. The small boat was flung about as though it weighed nothing at all. The waves broke over it and threatened at any moment to swamp it altogether. Grace and her father had to take a long, roundabout way to the wreck to get what little shelter was available.

2   This time, with more people to row, the journey did not take so long, and very soon the coble was on its way back with the remaining survivors. Later, the boat that had been lowered when the *Forfarshire* struck was picked up. Altogether, out of the sixty-three people who had sailed from Hull, only seventeen were left. Had it not been for Grace Darling, there would have been no survivors at all.

3   There were times when it seemed that they had been rowing for hours and when all the heart-bursting muscle-straining effort had resulted in no progress at all. But every now and then, as a huge wave raised the tiny boat aloft, they would catch sight of the helpless people on the rocks. The boat was by then visible to the survivors and some of them were waving. The sight spurred the brave girl and her equally valiant father to mightier efforts yet: and slowly, agonizingly, they drew near to what was left of the *Forfarshire*.

4   Immediately, Grace pleaded to be allowed to take the coble out in an attempt to rescue them. Her father was doubtful. A raging waste of water lay between the lighthouse and the victims of the wreck, and it seemed impossible to cross in the pitifully small coble. But to Grace, the impossibility did not matter. It was necessity that mattered. William Darling listened to her pleading, glanced across at the desperate, forlorn figures on the rocks and hesitated no longer.

5   Four men and a woman were taken on board, that being all that the coble could hold, and while Grace Darling ministered to the poor woman, William Darling and the men rowed the coble to the light-house, where the first survivors landed and were given into the efficient care of Mrs Darling.
    Grace and her father, together with two of the rescued men, then set off again to complete the rescue.

6   Near the wreck William Darling jumped onto the rocks and began to help the exhausted survivors while Grace managed the boat alone. William Darling found eight men and a woman with her two children, a boy and a girl. The poor little girl had died of exposure and all the others had suffered dreadfully.

Section D   Writing

You are one of the people who were rescued on that dangerous night. Tell the story of what happened to you in your own words.

19 DAN DUNDEE AND THE DUSTY D

Section A Arizona

☐ Read the sentences carefully and then answer the questions that follow.

a) Once upon a time, about a hundred years ago, in the Far West of America, in the very middle of a rather awful place called Arizona Territory, there was a ranch.

b) Of course, Arizona wasn't awful for everybody.

c) Very few places are awful for everybody.

d) Arizona, for example, was just the place to be if you were a rattlesnake.

e) You could guess that from the name of the place, because Arizona means 'The Dry Country' in Spanish, and when the first Spanish explorers crossed the Far West and wanted to think up names for the places they went through to put on their maps, 'The Dry Country' was the first thing they thought of to call it.

f) And it was precisely *because* it was dry that rattlesnakes liked it.

g) They liked to lie in the hot yellow-grey dust, or slither in and out of the yellow-grey rocks, and because they were yellow-grey, too, their enemies could not see them.

h) And the animals they preyed on for food couldn't see them either: if you were a desert rat, one moment you might be passing a dusty stick, and the next moment the dusty stick would have eaten you, because it wasn't a dusty stick at all, but a rattlesnake.

i) Arizona was also just the place if you were a Gila monster, or a tarantula spider, or a scorpion; which is why I think of Arizona as rather awful, because all those animals are poisonous, and not really my favourite animals at all.

j) Mind you, Arizona was, and is, very beautiful indeed; and if you could just look at it without worrying about snakes, spiders, scorpions, Gila monsters and so on, you would be right to think that it wasn't awful but exciting: its mountains soar up from vast yellow deserts, and at sunset its skies seem to catch fire, blazing orange and crimson and gold, fading at last to the colour of darkening plums before blackening into the blackest night you could ever imagine, so black that the stars seem not just white, but brilliant silver.

k) And it was in the very middle of all this, the hot yellow skies by day and the cold black skies by night, that the ranch stood that was called the Dusty D.

□ There are eleven sentences in this passage. They are concerned with these main subjects:
The ranch
Why the author doesn't like Arizona
Rattlesnakes
The climate of Arizona
What Arizona looks like

□ Copy the subjects down.

□ Against each one write the letters of the sentences that tell you about it. (Some letters will appear more than once, because some sentences are about more than one thing.)

□ Answer these questions by writing one or more sentences. Make the sentences up – do not quote them from the story.
1 Where is the Dusty D ranch?
2 Why does the author think Arizona is 'awful'?
3 Why do rattlesnakes like Arizona?
4 What is the climate of Arizona?
5 What does the landscape of Arizona look like?

Section B   The Dusty D

In this section fifteen words have been missed out.

☐ Read the passage and work out suitable words to go in the spaces.

☐ Write down the numbers of each space and, against each one, write the word you have chosen.

It was called the Dusty D because – well, you know by now why it was —1— Dusty, and the D came from the name of the man who —2— it, and that name was Dan Dundee. He had been a soldier in the American Civil War, and when the War had ended in 1865 he had ridden away from the battlefields in search of somewhere —3— and peaceful, somewhere where he wouldn't have to see people, because it had been a very terrible war —4—, and Dan Dundee had decided that he would like to be on his own for a while in a silent —5— place. And he rode for a thousand miles and more, west from Tennessee, through Arkansas and Oklahoma Territory, through Texas and New Mexico, until he came at last to the hot quiet —6— of Arizona, where, just because he liked it (which is a very good reason, after all), he —7—.
    And he built a one-roomed cabin in a place where there was a little —8—, and he irrigated a small patch of land with —9— from the creek, and grass grew from the moistened sandy —10—; and Dan Dundee worked very hard for five years, and at the end of five years the Dusty D wasn't quite so —11—, and he had a hundred cattle on his fairly green land. And partly because his ranch was now growing —12— quite rapidly, and partly because after five years he was beginning to feel he would like to have some people to —13— to again, he decided to take on two men to be ranch-hands, who would —14— with the five hundred cattle he —15— to buy as soon as he had the men to look after them.

Section C   Buckeye Bend

This section of the story has been divided into seven parts. The first part has been printed at the beginning, but the other six parts have been jumbled up.

☐ Read them through and work out the order they should be in.

☐ Write the numbers in that order.

So he saddled his horse, and he rode sixty miles, across the scrub-lands, over the Rio Verde, and through the hills at the foot of the Vulture Mountains until he came to the little town of Buckeye Bend, which wasn't much more than a church and a wooden hotel and a saloon and a general store and a livery stable and a gunsmith's and a barber shop and twenty-two little wooden houses where the people of Buckeye Bend sat and wondered how long it would take the railroad company to build a line to Buckeye Bend. Because until the railroad got there, Buckeye Bend would remain remarkably un-important, and nobody likes living in a remarkably unimportant place.

The railroad company kept promising; but nothing seemed to happen.

1   I looked inside, and there was something that looked very much like my hat, with carrots round it.'

'Lucky for you I happened along', said Dan Dundee (who was secretly hoping his steaks *had* been steaks, rather than shoes or table mats, or something), and he finished his beer, and the two men walked out of the hotel and into the yellow-grey-dusty street.

2   Which prompted Dan Dundee, who was quite a polite man, all in all, to say:

'Excuse me, but how long have you been a waiter?'

To which the waiter replied:

'I started this morning. They used to have a real waiter here, but he got sick and tired of waiting for the railroad to come, so he rode off last night.

3   Well, anyway, Dan Dundee got down from his horse, and gave it to the man at the livery stable to groom and feed, and he walked across to the wooden hotel and asked for the best room and he got the one with the washbasin in it, and he washed and cleaned his teeth and he brushed the yellow-grey Arizona dust from his clothes and he combed his hair, and he went downstairs and ordered two steaks in the dining room.

4   I'm a cowhand, but the man I worked for went out last week without his boots, and a scorpion got him in the foot, so that was that.'

And Dan Dundee said:

'There's a coincidence! I happen to be in town looking for a couple of cowhands, how'd you like to come and work for me?'

The waiter took off his apron.

'When can I start?' he said.

'It's a long ride,' warned Dan Dundee, 'and hard work when you get there.'

5   You may think that sounds greedy, you may feel that Dan Dundee was, not to put too fine a point on it, a bit of a pig; but you have to remember that in 1870 it took nearly two days to ride sixty miles, and Dan Dundee had missed two dinners, not to mention two lunches, so it was only reasonable, really, to want two steaks.

And he enjoyed his meal very much, except that the waiter dropped a potato into his lap and spilled beer onto his boots.

6   'Anything's better than waiting tables,' said the ex-waiter. 'I'm covered in soup, and I've only served three people so far. Also, I think the cook has roasted my hat.'

'What?' said Dan Dundee.

'I hung it next to the stove this morning,' explained the ex-waiter, 'and now it's disappeared, and there's a strange smell coming from the oven.'

Section D   Writing

---

1   You are the waiter. Tell the story of how you met Dan Dundee. Include in it, how you came to be working at the hotel and how you felt about it. Finish by describing how you and Dan set off for his ranch.

2   As Dan and the waiter ride along they talk about the ranch. Dan describes what he has done and what he plans to do. Write their conversation.

20 THE ASCENT OF EVEREST

Section A The roof of the world

In this section fifteen words have been missed out.

☐ Read the passage through and work out suitable words to fill each blank.

☐ Write the number of each blank and, against it, write the word you have chosen.

Between the wind-swept plateaux of Tibet and the deep mountain valleys of Nepal is the 'roof of the world'. Here rise the Himalayan

Mountains – the 'land of the snows'. And towering above all the mighty Himalayan —1— stands Mount Everest, at 8848 metres the highest point on earth.

Where Everest now soars above the clouds there was once a great sea. The mountains were formed between 7 and 25 million years ago, as the Indian sub-continent moved northwards to collide with Tibet. The Himalayas are still —2—, as the rocks beneath the Earth are forced upwards by the colossal pressure.

Snow and ice cover the rocky slopes and slow-moving glaciers grind their way down into distant valleys. Only in these —3— can plants and animals survive the extremes of the climate.

In the Khumbu Valley, in the shadow of Everest, live the Sherpas. These mountain people are used to the demands of altitude. They —4— invaluable help to climbers such as Edmund Hillary by acting as guides and porters. The Sherpas can follow the twisting mountain —5— for many hours without tiring. They grow crops of potatoes and corn and keep herds of yaks. Yaks are the mountain cattle of the Himalayas.

The Sherpas are Buddhists. And high in the mountains travellers are welcomed at —6— monasteries, where prayer wheels spin endlessly in the wind and prayer flags flutter on tall poles.

Hillary and his fellow climbers were entertained by Sherpa stories of the yeti, a mysterious —7— said to look like a large hairy ape. But its existence has never been proved.

Before the 1850s the Himalayas were almost —8— to the outside world. Few Europeans had ever made the long and difficult journey to Tibet and Nepal hidden beyond their wall of mountains.

At this time India was part of the British Empire. And the British government was —9— to know exactly how large India was. The man given this task was the Surveyor-General, George Everest.

A survey team travelled across India, using trigonometry to make their measurements. And as they worked their way into the —10— of the Himalayas, they saw far off a group of mountain peaks wreathed in cloud.

The survey party never got closer than 150 kilometres. Yet they had no doubt that these were the —11— mountains they had ever seen. Excitedly, they took their measurements. They could hardly believe their eyes, but it was true. The highest mountain was over 8800 metres high.

The surveyors —12— the local people, who told them the Tibetan names for the mountains – Changtse, Khumbutse, Nuptse, Lhotse and, greatest of them all, Chomolungma 'the Goddess Mother of the World'.

At first the new mountain was known simply as Peak XV, but in 1863 it was given the name Mount Everest. Its height was thought to be 8840 metres, but —13— measurements showed that it was in fact 29,028 feet or 8848 metres – unquestionably the highest mountain in the world.

No-one then thought of climbing Everest, for mountaineering had hardly —14—. In 1865 Edward Whymper (1840–1911) conquered the Matterhorn (4477 metres) in the Swiss Alps. He went on to explore the Andes Mountains of South America and in 1880 he climbed Chimborazo (6310 metres). Whymper studied the effects of 'mountain sickness' at high altitude and pioneered several mountaineering techniques.

One by one the European peaks were conquered. For a new —15—, climbers began to look eagerly towards the distant Himalayas and the mysterious Chomolungma.

Section B   The challenge

☐ Read the passage through carefully and then answer the questions that follow it.

Climbing Everest is difficult and dangerous. The climber must overcome deep snow, crevasses, walls of ice and sheer rock faces. He must face the perils of altitude and hope for a spell of good weather.

Above 6400 metres the thin air makes breathing difficult and each step demands a painful effort. Climbing at such heights, a man quickly becomes exhausted and he finds it hard to think clearly.

During the winter, from November to March, freezing winds howl around Everest. Plumes of snow stream from the summit and avalanches crash down the mountain. In early summer the monsoon winds bring blizzards to the Himalayas. Climbers can only venture on Everest just before or just after the monsoon.

Everest can be approached from the north, by way of Tibet, tackling the mountain by the North East Ridge. But most modern expeditions have taken the southern route through Nepal – a route which leads up the Khumbu Glacier and the Icefall.

Below the valley called the Western Cwm the way is blocked by a gigantic step, 600 metres high. This is the Icefall, a treacherous cascade of ice blocks, constantly shifting to reveal yawning crevasses.

Beyond the Icefall wide snow slopes lead up to the icy wall of the Lhotse Face, and above the wall is the point known as the South Col (7900 metres). The route to the summit lies along the snow crest of the South East Ridge – with a drop of thousands of metres on either side.

1 For each of these statements say whether it is true or false:
   a) Above 6400 metres climbing hurts your feet.
   b) The only times Everest can be climbed are the spring and the
       early autumn.
   c) The most popular route up Everest starts in Tibet.
2 Look at the picture of Everest and then answer these questions:
   a) What is Country A?
   b) What is Country B?

3 Match the following names to the letters on the map:

      North East Ridge
      South Col
      Icefall
      Summit
      Lhotse Face

Section C   Everest is climbed

This section has been divided up into seven parts. The first part is printed at the beginning, but the rest have been printed in the wrong order.

☐ Study them carefully and work out what the correct order is.

☐ Write the numbers in that order.

In 1953 a team of British and Commonwealth climbers began an attempt to climb Everest. By the end of April they had reached the Khumbu Icefall.

As they scrambled up through the Khumbu Icefall, the climbers marked the route with flags. Often these flags vanished overnight as the huge ice blocks shifted and yet another crevasse opened up. Many crevasses were too wide to jump across and were bridged by portable metal ladders. Climbers and Sherpas would then crawl over on their hands and knees.

Crampons and ice axes were essential, and often the weary porters needed handlines to help them clamber up among the ice boulders. Fortunately the going became less hazardous as they moved up the Western Cwm.

1   The weather was fine although the wind was unrelenting. On May 26 Bourdillon and Evans climbed to the South Summit – higher than any men before them. But it was too late to risk going further, for their start had been delayed by trouble with the oxygen apparatus. Reluctantly, they turned back. Now it was up to Hillary and Tenzing.

2   Throughout May groups of climbers toiled from one camp to the next, bringing up supplies and equipment. Camps 4 and 5 were pitched on the Cwm; while 6 and 7 were established on the steep Lhotse Face.

3   On May 28, Hillary and Tenzing moved up to Camp 9. Already they were firm friends. Hillary (33) had learned to climb in the New Zealand Alps and Tenzing (39) had run away from his Nepalese village home to become a mountaineer.

They spent an uncomfortable night, for the wind was so fierce that Hillary had to brace his feet against the ridge to stop the tent from being blown away. At 6.30 on May 29, after a breakfast of sardines, biscuits and lemon juice, they set off.

4   The assault parties moved steadily up from Camp 4 which was at 6470 metres and was also referred to as Advance Base Camp. They worked their way up to the South Col – a three day climb by way of Camps 5, 6 and 7. Beyond Camp 8 on the South Col there was to be a final assault camp, Camp 9, at a height of 8500 metres on the South East Ridge.

The climbers chosen to make the first attempt on the summit were Tom Bourdillon and Charles Evans. Using closed-circuit breathing apparatus, they would start from the South Col. The second pair, Hillary and Tenzing, would be using the open-circuit system and would have to spend a night at Camp 9, high on the Ridge itself. There they would change their oxygen bottles before their attempt on the summit.

5   For 15 minutes Hillary and Tenzing stood on top of the world. Hillary photographed the incredible view. Tenzing left chocolate, biscuits and sweets as an offering to the gods. As he posed, grinning, for Hillary's camera, the flags of the United Nations, Britain, Nepal and India fluttered from Tenzing's ice axe.

On their weary return to the South Col, they were met by their support team and soon the news was radioed all over the world. The abbot at Thyangboche heard the news in polite disbelief and congratulated Hillary and Tenzing on 'nearly reaching the summit of Chomolungma'.

6   Hillary led the way along the ridge to the South Summit. Beyond lay the final curving crest on which no man had yet set foot. To the right huge snow banks overhung a sheer drop; below the slope on the left was the great rock wall rising from the Western Cwm far below them.

Cutting steps with their ice axes, Hillary and Tenzing plodded upwards. Forced to skirt round a rock, they struggled up through a crevice. This last obstacle passed, Hillary cut a few more steps – and saw the ridge fall away in front of him. They had reached the summit. It was 11.30.

Section D Writing

Imagine that you are Tom Bourdillon. You keep a daily diary of the Everest expedition. Write the diary entries for these dates:

    May 25th
    May 26th
    May 28th

21 Bees

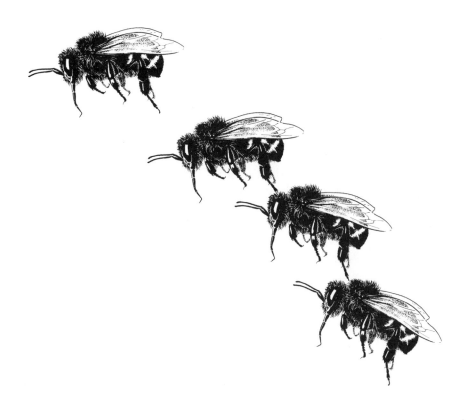

Section A   The hive

☐ Read the passage and then answer the questions that follow it.

A honey bee cannot live alone. It must live with other bees in a colony, or nest, if it is to survive.

Wild bees build their colonies in hollow trees or empty birds' nests. Wild bee colonies are easily destroyed by cold, strong winds and forest fires, and animals such as squirrels and bears.

Stone-age man used honey to sweeten his food. Cave paintings in Spain show that there was beekeeping, or apiculture, as long as 15,000 years ago.

But Stone-age man could not take the honey without destroying the nest. Today, beekeepers keep bees in wooden hives. The roof and the back of the hive lift off so that the beekeeper can take the honey without harming the bees.

The beehive is made up of a number of sections like boxes. In each box the beekeeper puts wooden frames with walls of thin wax already pressed out into *hexagonal* (six-sided) shapes. The worker bees build these shapes out into thousands of cells to make honey combs.

The queen bee lays her eggs in the cells in the middle of the frames in the bottom box. Around these are cells filled with nectar and pollen. The honey cells are on the edges of the frames. This first box is called the *brood chamber*.

The beekeeper wants to keep *his* honey separate in a special box or storehouse. This storehouse, or 'super' as the beekeeper calls it, is above the first box, the brood chamber. Between the two boxes there is a barrier grid, or 'queen excluder', to keep the queen and the drones out. Only the worker bees can get through it to leave their honey.

When the cells are filled, the worker bees cover each one with a wax lid. Gradually, the storehouse of honey is built up.

To harvest the honey, the beekeeper takes the frames out and puts them into an *extractor*, a special machine which takes the honey out of the comb. Afterwards, the beekeeper puts the frames back into the hive for the bees to fill with honey again.

1   What are the enemies of colonies of wild bees?
2   How do we know that there was beekeeping 15,000 years ago?
3   Find a word in the passage that describes this shape:

4   What should the labels on this diagram say? Write the letters and, against each one, write the correct label.

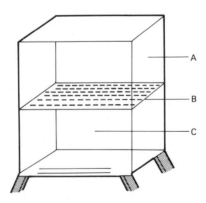

5   Find a word in the passage that means 'a machine that the beekeeper uses to get honey from the comb'.

Section B Queen, drones and workers

☐ Read the passage and then answer the questions that follow.

There are three kinds of bee: *queen, drones* and *worker bees.*

The *queen* is the largest. She is the only female bee to lay eggs. There is only one queen bee in a colony.

The *drones* are male bees. They have round clumsy bodies. The drones mate with the queen to fertilize her eggs so that there will be more bees. There are several hundred drones in each colony.

The *worker bees* are female. They clean the hive and fetch pollen and nectar from plants as food for the other bees.

The body of a bee is made up of a head, a chest (or *thorax*) and an *abdomen.*

On the head are three small *simple* eyes and two large *compound* eyes. Each compound eye is made up of many small eyes. On the front of the head are two feelers, or *antennae*, which the bee uses to smell and feel with. The bee's mouth is shaped into a narrow tube for sucking.

On the thorax are two pairs of wings and three pairs of legs.

In the abdomen of the female bee is the *poison gland*. This is the sting. The queen also has in her abdomen *ovaries* which produce eggs, and a sac called the *spermatheca*, which after mating is filled with sperm from the drones.

In the spring, the worker bees clean out the hive.

Now, the queen begins to lay her eggs. First, she investigates with her antennae whether the cells are clean. Then, if she is satisfied, she sticks her abdomen inside and lays a *fertilized egg* in every cell. She lays about 1,000 eggs every twenty-four hours, and on some days up to 2,500.

After three days, the egg hatches and a small *larva*, or grub, appears. It grows quickly and changes skin every twenty-four hours. After six days, the larva is fully grown. The worker bees then build a lid over the cell and the larva spins a web round itself.

The larva has now turned into a *pupa*, the next stage in its development. The beekeeper calls this a *sealed brood.*

Twenty to twenty-one days later, a new worker bee bites a hole in the wax lid, crawls out and at once begins to clean its body. It begs food from older bees by tapping them on the head.

For the first three weeks, the bee works at home in the hive. Then it becomes a field bee.

1 Which of these drawings shows:
  a worker bee
  a drone
  a queen?
Write the letter of each drawing and beside it write the correct label.

2 For each of these statements, say whether it is true or false.
  a) Male bees are drones.
  b) The bee's chest is called its *abdomen*.
  c) Bees have six eyes.
  d) Bees have two different types of eye.
  e) Bees smell with their antennae.
  f) The female bee cannot sting.
  g) A queen will lay eggs only in a clean cell.
  h) A queen may lay as many as 100 eggs an hour.

3   The diagram that follows shows the stages in the development of a bee in the cell. The cells have been put in the wrong order. Write the numbers of the cells in the correct order. Beside each number explain what the drawing shows.

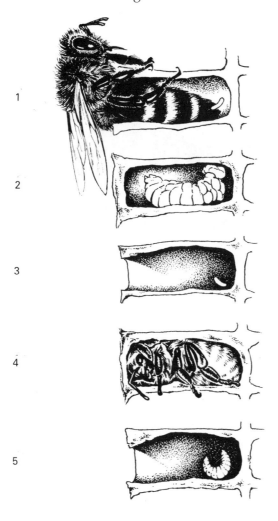

Section C   Nectar and pollen

In this passage, ten words have been missed out.

☐ Read the passage and work out what the missing words should be.

☐ Write the number of each blank and against it write the word you have chosen.

Bees feed on *pollen* and *nectar*.

The worker bees collect *pollen* from the male catkins of hazel and pussy willow, and from flowers. The bees collect the pollen in small baskets, or 'pollen breeches', on their —1— —2—. Pollen also sticks to the small fine hairs which cover the bee's body.

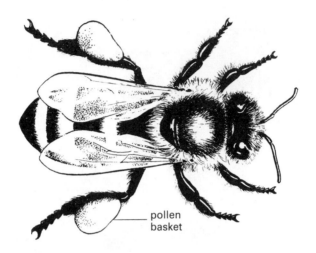

pollen basket

While the bees are collecting pollen, the pollen is carried from male to female flowers. This is called *pollination*. In this way many plants are fertilized and seeds for new plants formed.

When the bee's pollen —3— are full, she flies home to the hive. Since a single colony needs over twenty-five kilos of —4— a year, the worker bees have to make a great many flights.

Bees can find nectar in most flowers. The bees suck it up with their tube-like mouths. The nectar then passes into the —5— —6—, or honey stomach, and there it begins to be made into honey.

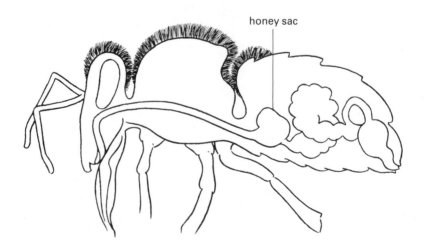

honey sac

In the hive, the nectar is brought up and much of the water in it evaporates.

When the bees find a good place with unusually sweet and plentiful nectar, they tell each other by doing either a —7— *dance* or a *wagging* —8—.

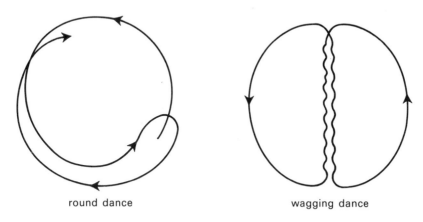

round dance   wagging dance

Worker bees that collect pollen and —9— are called *field bees*. After about three weeks' work as field bees, their wings are worn out and they —10—.

Section D Writing

A younger brother, who is six, hates bees and keeps asking you to kill them for him. You decide that if he understood more about bees he might be less frightened of them. What would you tell him? Write out your explanation.

What happens next?

While we are reading stories we often have a guess about what will happen next. In this section that is what you will be asked to do. It contains five stories. Each one is divided into parts. After each part there are questions asking you to guess what you think will happen in the next part. So that people are not tempted to cheat, all the parts are jumbled up and numbered. You will be told the number of the part you have to read.

1 The Balaclava Story

Tony and Barry both had one. I reckon half the kids in our class had them. But I didn't. My mum wouldn't even listen to me.

'You're not having a balaclava! What do you want a balaclava for in the middle of summer?'

I must have told her about ten times why I wanted a balaclava.

'I want one so I can join the Balaclava Boys.'

'Go and wash your hands for tea, and don't be so silly.'

I knew exactly the kind of balaclava I wanted. One just like Tony's – a sort of yellowy-brown.

His dad had given it to him because of his earache. Mind you, he didn't like wearing it at first.

At school he'd give it to Barry to wear and get it back before home-time. But all the other lads started asking if they could have a wear of it, so Tony took it back and said from then on nobody but him could wear it – not even Barry.

Barry told him he wasn't bothered because he was going to get a balaclava of his own, and so did some of the other lads.

And that's how it started – the Balaclava Boys.

a) *Who were the Balaclava Boys?*
b) *What do you think they did?*
c) *Why did he want to join them?*

2 | How the Whale Became

Now God had a little back-garden. In this garden he grew carrots, onions, beans and whatever else he needed for his dinner. It was a fine little garden. The plants were in neat rows, and a tidy fence kept out the animals. God was pleased with it.

One day as he was weeding the carrots he saw a strange thing between the rows. It was no more than an inch long, and it was black. It was like a black shiny bean. At one end it had a little root going into the ground.

'That's very odd,' said God. 'I've never seen one of these before. I wonder what it will grow into.'

So he left it growing.

Next day, as he was gardening, he remembered the little shiny black thing. He went to see how it was getting on. He was surprised. During the night it had doubled its length. It was now two inches long, like a shiny black egg.

Every day God went to look at it, and every day it was bigger. Every morning, in fact, it was just twice as long as it had been the morning before.

When it was six feet long, God said:

'It's getting too big. I must pull it up and cook it.'

But he left it a day.

Next day it was twelve feet long and far too big to go into any of God's pans.

So what do you think God did?

The Lion in the Sewer

Many years ago, young Frank Bostock brought his menagerie to the three days' Onion Fair in Birmingham. In the menagerie was a lion called Nero. Nero was a beautiful creature, big, sleek, and tawny, with a great, chubby head and strong shoulders, covered with a handsome dark mane. A real king of beasts – young Frank Bostock was very proud of him.

Well, the menagerie was set up on the fair-ground, with the animal cages arranged on three sides of an open square, so that people could walk all the way round. And on the fourth side of the square was the show-front, made of cloth that was coloured and gilded, and had huge pictures of animals painted all over it. And, on a platform under the show-front sat eight bandsmen, wearing scarlet tunics and leopard-skin hats, and playing away on their brass instruments to attract the crowds.

Young Frank Bostock walked round his show, examining everything, to make sure that all was in order. All was in order, and he felt well pleased.

'I think, though,' says he, 'we'll shift Nero into a larger cage. He's grown too big for the one he's in.'

So his men brought up another cage, and put a big chunk of meat in it, and opened the doors of both cages, and tried to persuade Nero to go into the new one.

But something frightened Nero; perhaps it was the noise of all the thousands of people who had come to see the fair, though he should have been used to fair-ground noises by this time; or perhaps it was some little thing, like a piece of broken glass, glittering in the sun, that he didn't understand. At any rate, *something* frightened him, and instead of going into the new cage, he made a sudden dash out of the cage he was in; and, before anyone could stop him, he had rushed right out of the menagerie, and into the open fair-ground.

And what do you think happened?

The Fossil Snake

The truck stood in the yard loaded with stone that was to be used for building a wall. The young driver let down the flap and then winched up the body of the truck carelessly high, so that the stone shot down with a noise like a falling cliff.

'Idiot,' said Rob's father. 'You'll have smashed half of it.'

'So what! Stone's stone.'

'And rubble's rubble, but I ordered large pieces. Small bits are no good.'

While his father was telling the driver just what he thought of him, Rob was clambering round the edge of the heap.

'Here's a splendid big piece broken in two.'

'Careless idiot!' said his father as the truck was driven off.

'And look, Daddy, what's on the inside!'

Where the rock had split, on one surface was a raised shape like a coiled-up snake, on the other a hollow mould that had fitted over it.

'What can it be?'

'It's a fossil snake. Millions of years ago it was frozen in an ice age, buried in an avalanche perhaps, and then hundreds of thousands of years later there was a hot age with earthquakes and volcanoes of boiling rock, and the lava covered the frozen snake and turned into stone and afterwards there was another ice age and the rocks were cracked up and moved down by glaciers, and ultimately came to rest where they were quarried. And there it stayed till today when the stone was smashed. It's a wonderful specimen. Look, you can even see the patterns of the scales on its body.'

Rob ran loving fingers round the diminishing coils.

'Can I keep it?'

What answer did Rob get, and what makes you think so?

Ice

In some places the snow was no thicker than a finger but in others it came higher than a wellington boot. Whichever it was Jimmy hated it.

It wasn't even white any more – not all over anyway. Some of it was just slush. This was caused by feet that crunched through it and hands that scooped it together for throwing. And toboggans.

Toboggans had worn it away most of all. Including Jimmy's toboggan. If you could call the thing *Jimmy's* toboggan. Teddy's toboggan more like. Or maybe Teddy-Pete-and-Kit's toboggan. Anybody would think *their* Dad had made it. Anybody would think it belonged to *them* or to some kid who'd lent it out for the day. You wouldn't think it belonged to Jimmy. How could it belong to Jimmy when he was the only one who got scared? Jimmy was sick of the toboggan and sick of the snow and most of all he was sick of being Jimmy.

He looked around him miserably. Martin's Hill was different from the park where they usually went. Their normal park was vast and flat like a pitch for people with seven-league football boots. Also it was safe . . . unlike Martin's Hill. Martin's Hill had a slope that took you to breakneck speed before you could even catch your breath. It had ledges and dips and gullies. It had stretches of ice like a skid-pan with trees and lamp-posts as obstacles. Martin's Hill was a somersaulting, head-on collision-course for mad kids on runaway sledges.

So why was he the *only* kid who got frightened?

He thought of Teddy. Teddy crouched on the toboggan jockeystyle and treated each ride as if it were a frost-bitten Grand National which he just managed to win in the final furlong. Pete lay back like a racing-driver. Even Kit skimmed the ground, flat-out.

Still, at least for the moment Teddy and Peter and Kit were out of sight over the hill. They had stared after him when he stomped off.

'Hey, where are you going?' Pete called. 'It's your turn, Jimmy.'

'He's just going to the bog,' suggested Teddy.

'The bog?' Kit exclaimed. 'What – just before his turn?'

Jimmy hadn't heard Teddy's reply. If he made a reply. Probably already they were arguing over who took his place on the toboggan. On *his* toboggan. But if it was his toboggan why was he in such a funk about it?

They were older than him, of course. In two or three years' time maybe he would be just as reckless . . . maybe. Anyway, in a day or two the snow would be gone and the problem would be over . . . until the roller-skating season started or tree-climbing began or it came round to summer and jumping off the top board at the swimming-pool. Each of these left him dizzy with fear.

Perhaps you were just born brave. Or perhaps being brave was something you could get good at bit by bit. Like today . . . was there some small risk he could take which he could build on gradually till by next winter it really would be his toboggan? There were no kids on this side of the slope. It was steep and long but too straightforward to be popular for tobogganing. Once you were at the bottom it took an age to get back to the top. Also the slope ended at the boating pool.

In summer the pool was overhung with leaves and full of coloured rowing-boats and pedal-boats and canoes like dodgem-cars in a floating fun-fair. These vanished in the autumn. Teddy said the park-keepers buried them like Viking treasure-ships and dug them up again in the spring. Jimmy knew this wasn't true. It was just Teddy being funny. By winter the pond was just a pond – half an acre of space surrounded by gaunt trees with the level of the ice about three feet below the pond's edge. Perhaps some of the water had gone underground with the boats, Jimmy thought bitterly.

Then he had his idea.

a) *What do you think of Jimmy?*
b) *What do you suppose his idea was?*
c) *Do you think it will work?*

6   The creatures walked round Whale-Wort, looking at him. His skin was so shiny they could see their faces in it.

'Leave it,' suggested Ostrich. 'And wait till it dies down.'

'But it might go on growing,' said God. 'Until it covers the whole earth. We shall have to live on its back. Think of that.'

'I suggest,' said Mouse, 'that we throw it into the sea.'

God thought.

'No,' he said at last. 'That's too severe. Let's just leave it for a few days.'

After three more days, God's house was completely flat, and Whale-Wort was as long as a street.

'Now,' said Mouse, 'it is too late to throw it into the sea. Whale-Wort is too big to move.'

But God fastened long thick ropes round him and called up all the creatures to help haul on the ends.

'Hey!' cried Whale-Wort. 'Leave me alone.'

'You are going into the sea,' cried Mouse. 'And it serves you right. Taking up all this space.'

'But I'm happy!' cried Whale-Wort again. 'I'm happy just lying here. Leave me and let me sleep. I was made just to lie and sleep.'

'Into the sea!' cried Mouse.

'No!' cried Whale-Wort.

'Into the sea!' cried all the creatures. And they hauled on the ropes. With a great groan, Whale-Wort's root came out of the ground. He began to thresh and twist, beating down houses and trees with his long root, as the creatures dragged him willy-nilly through the countryside.

At last they got him to the top of a high cliff. With a great shout they rolled him over the edge and into the sea.

'Help! Help!' cried Whale-Wort. 'I shall drown! Please let me come back on land where I can sleep.'

'Not until you're smaller!' shouted God. 'Then you can come back.'

'But how am I to get smaller?' wept Whale-Wort, as he rolled to and fro in the sea. 'Please show me how to get smaller so that I can live on land.'

God bent down from the high cliff and poked Whale-Wort on the top of his head with his finger.

'Ow!' cried Whale-Wort. 'What was that for? You've made a hole. The water will come in.'

What do you think God answered?

7   Rob was choking with anger, meaning to let fly at his father, but then he remembered that the Museum's piece was very much larger,

that his father did not know where he had hidden the fossil and anyway he couldn't believe he would do a thing like that. He remembered the sounds in the night and slipped quietly back into his bedroom to think about it. While he was dressing, he decided it would be better not to say anything. It is always better to have secret ideas. You never know what grown-ups will forbid.

At breakfast his mother said, 'I must buy some mouse traps. I never heard such a chattering and squealing as they made last night. They sounded as if they'd all gone mad. Could there be a weasel in the house?'

'I never heard of weasels in houses but this one is so old perhaps they'd hardly recognize it as a house and mistake it for a quarry or part of the landscape. Lots of nice cracks everywhere.'

'If it was a weasel, how would you catch it?'

'Why should you want to? It's catching mice for us. When it has eaten them all it will go hunting somewhere else.'

Rob listened to this conversation between his parents with relief. He was glad that traps or poison would not be ordered, because he had his own notion of what was going on.

Just to make sure he asked carelessly, 'What else eats mice beside weasels?'

'Owls and cats, but they'd hardly be under the floor boards.' His father was eating, and answered between mouthfuls. 'That goes for herons too. Hedgehogs would if they found a nestful of babies; dogs if they were starving; grass snakes, though I think they prefer frogs. Any kind of snake I daresay. Is there any more coffee, dear? Then I must get on with the wall. Rob, will you come and help?'

Rob nodded. 'In a minute I will,' and he went upstairs.

Where was Rob going, and why?

8   My mum wasn't back from work, thank goodness, so as soon as I shut the front door, I put my hand down the sleeve of my coat for the balaclava. There was nothing there. That was funny, I was sure I'd put it down that sleeve.

I tried down the other sleeve, and there was still nothing there. Maybe I'd got the wrong coat – no, it was my coat all right. Oh, blimey, I must've lost it while I was running home.

I was glad in a way. I only hoped nobody had seen it drop out, but, oh, I was glad to be rid of it.

Mind you, I dreaded going to school next morning. Norbert would have probably reported it by now. Well, I wasn't going to own up. I didn't mind the cane – it wasn't that, but if you owned up, you had to go up on the stage in front of the whole school.

Then I thought about my mum. What she'd say if she knew I'd been stealing.

I went into the kitchen and peeled some potatoes for my mum. She was ever so pleased when she came in from work, and said I must have known she'd brought me a present.

'Oh, thanks. What have you got me?'

She gave me a paper bag, and when I opened it I couldn't believe my eyes – a blooming balaclava.

'There you are, now you won't be left out and you can stop making my life a misery.'

'Thanks, mum.'

If only my mum knew she was making my life a misery. The balaclava she'd bought me was just like the one I'd pinched.

I felt sick – I didn't want it. I couldn't wear it now. If I did, everybody would say it was Norbert Lightowler's. Even if they didn't, I just couldn't wear it. I wouldn't feel it was mine.

If he wasn't going to wear it, what do you think he did with it?

---

9   Every now and then a man would come running to say that Nero's great head had been seen poking up from this man-hole or that, with his eyes glaring, and his ears flat, and his lips lifted in a snarl – people were imagining that they could see him everywhere! And every now and then, a policeman would come up and tell Frank that there were a hundred thousand people on the fair-ground, half mad with fear, and threatening a riot; and that he must, he simply *must*, do something!

So young Frank decided that he *would* do something. If he couldn't catch Nero, he could at least quieten the people by pretending to catch him. So he chose out one or two of his most trusted animal keepers, and told them what he intended to do.

The keepers went back to the menagerie, and put another lion, a very old and quiet one, called Punch, into a shifting den. The den had a partition in it, worked by a spring, and Punch was behind this partition. Then the men covered the den over completely with thick canvas, so that no one could see Punch inside; and after that, they hoisted it up, lion and all, on to a wagon drawn by two horses.

Away went the wagon, rumbling through the city, and out through the suburbs, followed by a huge crowd of excited people. When they reached the brook, the den was taken off the wagon, and placed in front of the man-hole down which Nero had disappeared.

Meanwhile, some distance away, one of the lion trainers, Orenzo, entered the sewer by another man-hole. Orenzo was carrying a strange assortment of weapons with him: a revolver, a bundle of fireworks – such as Roman Candles and crackers – a frying-pan, and a thick stick. And he also took Marco, Frank Bostock's boarhound, with him.

Slowly, slowly, Orenzo and Marco crawled along the sewer in the direction of the brook. Orenzo was making as much noise as he possibly could, setting off his fireworks, banging with the frying-pan, beating the sides of the tunnel with his thick stick, and urging on Marco to bark and growl his loudest.

'Well, certainly,' the waiting crowds told each other, 'something's happening down there!' For all this noise was echoing like thunder along the low sewer tunnel, and the thunderous echoes were drawing nearer and nearer to the brook.

Suddenly the noise stopped. There was a moment's complete silence; and then two quick revolver shots. That was the signal young Frank Bostock was waiting for. The men in charge of the shifting den touched the spring, there was a sharp click, the partition fell in, the men snatched the canvas off the den – and there stood a lion, plain for all to see!

a) *What had they done?*
b) *What was the problem?*

10   I don't know what came over me. As soon as I saw that balaclava lying there on the floor, I decided to pinch it. I couldn't help it. I just knew that this was my only chance. I'd never pinched anything before.

I picked it up, went to my coat, and put it in the pocket. At least I tried to put it in the pocket but it bulged out, so I pushed it down the inside of the sleeve. Then I went back to the classroom and as I was going in I realized what I'd done.

I'd stolen a balaclava.

I didn't even know whose it was, but as I stood in the doorway I couldn't believe I'd done it. If only I could go back – in fact, I thought I would, but Mr Garnett told me to hurry up and sit down.

I thought home-time would never come, but when the bell did ring I got out as quick as I could.

I was going to put the balaclava back before anybody noticed, but as I got to the cloakroom I heard Norbert Lightowler shout out that someone had pinched his balaclava.

Nobody took much notice, thank goodness, and I heard Tony say to him that he'd most likely lost it.

Norbert said he hadn't but he went off to make sure it wasn't in the classroom.

I tried to be all casual and took my coat, but I didn't dare put it on in case the balaclava popped out of the sleeve, and said tarah to Tony.

'Tarah, Tony, see you tomorrow.'

'Yeh, tarah.'

Oh, it was good to get out in the open air. I couldn't wait to get home and get rid of that blooming balaclava.

What do you think he did when he got home?

---

11   While he was asleep he had grown back to the length of a street and the fatness of a ship with two funnels.

He rose to the surface as fast as he could and began to blow. Soon he was back down to the size of a lorry. But soon, too, he felt like another sleep. He took a deep breath and sank to the bottom.

When he awoke he was back to the length of a street.

This went on for years. It is still going on.

As fast as Whale-Wort shrinks with blowing, he grows with sleeping. Sometimes, when he is feeling very strong, he gets himself down to the size of a motor-car. But always, before he gets himself down to the size of a cucumber, he remembers how nice it is to sleep. When he wakes, he has grown again.

He longs to come back on land and sleep in the sun, with his root in the earth. But instead of that, he must roll and blow, out on the wild sea. And until he is allowed to come back on land, the creatures call him just Whale.

12 | 'It doesn't matter,' Jimmy said.

To their surprise he wasn't in tears. There was a grin on his face almost.

'I wasn't much good at it anyway,' he added.

'All you needed was practice,' said Teddy.

'And you won't get any now,' said Pete. 'Thanks to us.'

'Well, we didn't do it on purpose,' Kit protested. 'Must've been the design of the thing.'

'Leave off,' grated Teddy. 'We wrecked it. Simple as that. We shouldn't all have ridden it together and that was your idea if I remember rightly.'

'Forget it,' said Jimmy. 'It was funny, really.'

'Funny?' they echoed.

'In a way.'

But he didn't tell them in what way and they didn't ask. They were too relieved to have him smiling about it as he helped them gather up the pieces.

13 | The Director frowned and tapped on his desk.

'No, no, Stephen. I won't have that sort of dealing in this Museum. You know it could be worth much more.'

'Yes, I do. But it ought to be in safe keeping.' Stephen turned to Rob again.

'Where will you keep it, chum?' The impertinence of 'chum' annoyed Rob.

'I'll take good care of it,' was all he said, as he put it back in his satchel.

Rob was proud and overjoyed to have something so precious. Every time he looked at it or touched it, he was astonished at its mystery and perfection and at its unimaginable age. A thing like that must have magic. Things which came alive in the beginning of the world must have had enough energy bottled up in them to make everything else happen that developed from them afterwards.

He took the fossil upstairs to his bedroom. He wanted it to be a secret, and nobody else to see or touch it when he wasn't there, so he pushed it underneath the radiator. If it was a real snake it would like that, he thought. When they escaped from zoos they were always found in airing cupboards or among the hot pipes.

'There,' he said, stroking it. 'Have a nice warm up.'

Then he thought he would go and look for more fossils. Who knows, he might find a fish, or a fern, or even the skeleton of a pterodactyl. But he found nothing else.

He had done a heavy day's work, so that after supper he shivered with tiredness.

'You'd better go to bed,' said his mother. 'It's coldish this evening. I'll turn the central heating up a little and you can be snug.'

Before getting into bed, he pulled out the stone for a last look. It was warm on top, but underneath it was still cold. It must get warm right through before anything would happen, he found himself thinking.

a) *What did he want to happen?*
b) *What do you think did happen?*

---

14   It was not Nero of course, it was Punch, but the watching crowd couldn't know that. And sleepy old Punch was playing his part well; for though he had been peacefully snoozing under his canvas covering, the revolver shots had roused him, and he had leaped up with a roar. Now he was actually running to and fro in the shifting den, and lashing his tail – the very image of a ferocious, newly-captured beast!

A great shout went up. 'The've got him! They've got him! They've got the lion!'

In triumphal procession the shifting den was taken back to the menagerie. Orenzo and Marco came up out of the sewer, and Orenzo was carried shoulder-high behind the wagon, amid the cheers of the excited onlookers. That afternoon, over forty thousand people swarmed into the menagerie, and filed past the cage of the mildly surprised old Punch, the supposed fierce lion that had escaped and been captured again. Never had the menagerie done such business! Money was rolling in, but – *Nero was still in the sewer!*

All that night, and all the night after that, young Frank Bostock could not sleep. Having placed armed sentries at the man-hole by the brook, he spent miserable hours of darkness, going round all the other man-holes in the city; watching, listening, but hearing nothing.

He felt simply terrible! And, on Saturday afternoon, which was the last afternoon of the three days' fair, he went to the Chief Constable, and told him the whole story. At first, the Chief Constable was very angry; but by and by, he calmed down, and said he supposed young Frank had acted for the best. Then together they thought out a plan for the recapture of Nero.

In the small hours of Sunday morning, when all the town was sleeping, two hundred men, policemen and menagerie hands, all sworn to secrecy, assembled in the big menagerie tent. Every man was armed; some with pistols, some with rifles, and some with crowbars, clubs, and carving knives.

Silently the men stole off to their appointed places along the sewers. Every exit was manned, and a shifting den was placed in position at the man-hole down which, three days ago, Nero had disappeared. Then, with three companions, and the boarhound, Marco, young Frank entered the dark and slimy sewer, and began crawling cautiously forward on hands and knees, for there was no room to stand upright.

By and by, Marco gave a sharp bark, followed by a throaty growl; and away in the darkness ahead gleamed two greenish-red eyes. Nero! Young Frank sent one of the men back with the news; and other trainers immediately lowered themselves into other man-holes, to which ropes with slip-knots were also fastened.

Firing off blank cartridges and Roman Candles, Frank and his two companions crawled nearer and nearer to those gleaming eyes, hoping that Nero would turn and retreat to the entrance by which he had come in, and where the shifting den was waiting for him.

But the gleaming eyes did not move: more blank cartridges, a real cascade of Roman Candles, furious growls and barks from Marco. Not a sound, not a movement ahead – the eyes still gleamed in the same place out of the darkness.

Young Frank, deeply puzzled, was considering what next to do, when the valiant Marco lost patience. Bristling and growling furiously, he dashed forward; and there, in that evil-smelling darkness, a ferocious battle raged between dog and lion. Roarings and barkings, growlings, snarlings and howlings, echoed back through the narrow tunnels; the demented Nero lashing out with all his panic strength, the valiant Marco returning again and again to the attack. Only when slashed, bitten, and bleeding from a dozen wounds, and almost at his last gasp, did Marco come crawling back to Frank Bostock for protection. Frank at once told one of his men to take him up to the surface, and have his wounds attended to.

Now there remained in the sewer young Frank and one other man – and ahead of them lurking in darkness, the infuriated Nero.

a) *If you were Frank, what would you do now?*
b) *What do you think he did?*

15   A pool empty of water. He still didn't know what the park-keepers did with the boats in winter but he knew what happend to the pond. They drained it.

The toboggan was what had been broken. One runner had snapped completely and the other was bent. The chassis had come apart. Sheepishly Teddy and Pete and Kit got to their feet.

'Maybe . . . maybe your Dad could sort of repair it,' said Pete brushing himself down.

Teddy shook his head.

'No. We've wrecked it. Have to be re-built completely.'

'Couldn't have been very well made,' Kit snorted. 'I mean it wasn't that much of a crash.'

'Shut up,' Teddy snapped. 'We've wrecked it, that's all. Sorry Jim. I'll tell your Dad it was us.'

How do you think Jimmy replied – and why?

16   'There's a lion loose! A *lion!* . . . There *is*. I tell you! Oh, oh, here he comes! . . . Run for your lives! . . . Run! Run! Run!'

All those thousands of people on the fair-ground were shouting and screaming and running in all directions!

Poor Nero, more frightened than ever at all the hub-bub, tore straight across the fair-ground, and out at the gates, and away through the streets of the city. Men, women, and children fled before him, the women dropping their shopping baskets, the business men losing their hats and their attaché cases in their panic, the shop-keepers slamming and bolting their doors, the policemen running and blowing their whistles, men in carts urging their horses at a gallop down side-streets – the whole city was in the wildest confusion.

The streets behind Nero were crowded with shouting people, but the streets in front of him were emptied as if by magic; and on and on he ran, right through the city, and through the suburbs, and into the country, till he came to a small brook, and into that brook he jumped – and disappeared!

What had happened? Just this. Under the waters of that small brook was a hole that led into the town sewers, and Nero had dropped right through this hole. And here he was now, wandering about underground through the sewer tunnels, that ran for miles and miles beneath the town.

At intervals along these tunnels, were the man-holes, or openings, for workmen to go down and inspect the drains; and, whenever Nero came to one of these man-holes, he let out a loud roar. Very soon an enormous crowd of people had gathered along the brook-side, listening to Nero's progress down below, as he stopped at every man-hole, and sent up deep-chested roar after roar, that echoed along the enclosed space of the sewer tunnels, so that the very earth itself seemed to be roaring, and the listeners grew half wild with terror.

Nero was not really a savage animal. Frank Bostock who, young as he was, was known to be one of the greatest animal trainers then living, could usually do anything with him. He would pat and fondle the great chubby head, tickle the big sleek body (Nero loved to be tickled) and get him to take food out of his hand. But now that Nero was so excited and terrified, young Frank knew that there would be no doing anything with him, and that it would be impossible to entice him out of those sewers.

What on earth was to be done?

If you were Frank Bostock, what would you have done?

---

17 This very instant he could make a start at being brave . . .

The pond's surface stretched away like a frosted window laid flat. He couldn't tell how thick the ice was on top or how deep the water was beneath. But he could try it out. What was it he had to do? That student, Miss Dixon, had taught a lesson on it long ago in October when his own teacher had been away and he'd spent the day in the top class with Teddy and Pete and Kit.

'. . . Think about it,' Miss Dixon said. 'What part of you is taking all your weight? Kit?'

'Your feet.'

'Right. Now does that mean the weight is pressing down on a big area or a little area?'

'A little area,' said Pete.

'Depends on the size of your feet,' said Godfrey. 'I mean – Jimmy's got little dimity feet but Fatty Rosewell in the secondary school, he's got feet like frying-pans.'

Everyone laughed including Miss Dixon.

'That's true,' she said. 'People's feet do come in different sizes. My

own are quite big, you'll notice. But there's never that much difference. The point is that a lot of heaviness on a little bit of space puts on
too much pressure. That's what cracks the ice. So what can you do
about it?'

'Diet,' said Godfrey.

Everyone laughed again. Some kids overdid it a bit which was
what Godfrey was after.

'That would take rather a long time,' said Miss Dixon briskly, 'and
it might not work because it's not easy to shrink some parts of your
body. Your head, for example.'

That shut Godfrey up. Teddy raised his hand.

'What about spreading out your weight?' he suggested. 'I mean
you can't do much about how heavy you are but you could sort of
alter the area it's pressing on.'

'How could you do that?' Godfrey demanded.

'Well . . . you could go down on your hands and knees.'

'That's right,' said Pete. 'You lie on your feet and slide yourself
over the ice.'

'Exactly,' Miss Dixon agreed. 'Smashing, Teddy! Well done, Pete!
The important thing is to spread out your weight as much as you can.
So if you *do* see someone who's plunged through the ice and is
struggling and there's no one else around to help, then *crawl* over the
ice until you're close enough to give them something to catch on
to – a piece of rope or your coat or the branch of a tree. Okay? Don't
try to reach them standing up. You'd just go through the ice yourself.
You've got to act fast because a person can't live very long in freezing
water. Also the person might be a non-swimmer, of course. But you
mustn't hurry it whatever you do.'

That was Miss Dixon's advice.

So how do you think Jimmy proceeded with his idea?

18   The next day was like any other, but Rob was haunted by an
undercurrent of excitement. At night he looked at his stone. It was
warm all through. He put it carefully back.

'Hatch out, my lovely,' he said, not knowing if he was pretending
or believing. He hovered round it for a while, his heart beating. At last
he got into bed.

He was just getting warm in bed and dropping off to sleep when
he was startled by a slithering noise. It was not that it was loud, but it
was not a sound he recognized. Could it have been his dressing gown

slipping off the bed? No one would wake up for that. He switched on the light. The dressing gown was on the floor, so perhaps that was all. He went to sleep again, and not surprisingly dreamed of snakes.

It was a disturbed night. Never before had the mice made such a noise, scurrying and squeaking, and after their scutter above the ceiling just over his bed, there followed a very queer sound like someone softly stroking the joists with sandpaper. Rob lay wondering. The house felt different, as if something beside themselves had come to live in it. In the end he slept late and only woke when he was called to breakfast. His first act when he got out of bed was to look at his fossil. He pulled the stone out from under the radiator and was at first astonished and then enraged to see that there was no fossil snake, but only a shallow groove where it had been coiled. His father must have changed his mind and taken the fossil for the Museum and brought back the hollow mould to put in its place while he was asleep. How dared he?

What has happened?

---

19   'No, I never lost it at all. Some fool had shoved it down the sleeve of my raincoat.'

---

20   No. That would be chicken too. He slithered forward, shivering at first from fright not cold. For a while he was protected by the thick woollens his Mum insisted he wore . . . till wetness began to seep through here-and-there bringing with it a bone-aching chill. Half-sliding, half-crawling and despite Miss Dixon's instructions, he increased his speed. Each second he expected a sudden splitting and a rush of water. And shock. The shock itself could kill you. Some kid in the class had said that. And supposing you got trapped under the ice – coughing and spluttering to death in a frigid darkness? Jimmy whimpered at the thought of it. How far had he got to go? He lifted his head to look and the whimper died away. He had reached the centre of the pond already.

He could hardly believe it. He shifted to look behind him. From the pond's stone rim to where he lay was a trail of disturbed snow, ice-bound underneath. There was no hint of a crack. Miss Dixon had been right. Or was the water frozen so solid that he needn't have been so cautious? After all people did actually *skate* on ice. This ice felt as solid as rock apart from the crunching eggshell sound and he'd got used to that. Maybe . . . maybe *he* could stand up like a skater. Did he dare?

With treetops and diving-boards also in mind Jimmy inch-by-inched to his feet. His teeth were gritted, his fists clenched. To his astonishment he found he was sweating. Once, almost there, he slipped. Just in time he recovered his balance. Finally, arms spread like a high-wire walker, he was upright. He wanted to grin, but didn't, in case that was enough to topple him. All he had to do now was settle how he got back – walking or crawling, over new ice or over the ice he'd already tested. He swivelled, trying to decide which, and at the top of the slope something caught his eye.

Far off on the hill's crest three kids were getting a toboggan into position. One straddled the front, one the rear and the third squeezed into the middle. Three boys on one sledge? Crazy, Jimmy thought. Then he saw it was Teddy and Pete and Kit. He saw them using their legs like oars as they propelled the toboggan forward. Once it was on the move they tucked up their knees and hunched their shoulders, urging it faster. Jimmy stared in horror.

a) *Why, do you think Jimmy stared in horror?*
b) *What do you imagine happened next?*

21   Crouched on hands and knees, with his assistant lying almost alongside, but just a little behind him, all that Frank could see of Nero were those two greenish-red eyes, that glared and gleamed, but never moved.

Why did Nero not move? He *must* be got on the move somehow! The first thing that Frank did was to take off his big jack-boots, and put them on his hands and arms, as a protection against Nero's teeth and claws. Then, inch by inch, he crawled forward.

Still Nero did not move. He just gave a deep, angry growl, that was all. Frank was now so close to him that he could feel Nero's hot breath on his face. If he could but have stood upright, he would have had more chance; but, crouched as he was, his head was at Nero's mercy. If now Nero should lash out with one of his heavy paws, he could split Frank's head open like an egg-shell.

'Quick, the pail! Put the pail over my head,' Frank whispered to his assistant.

This was a large iron pail in which they were carrying their blank cartridges. The man clapped it over Frank's head like a helmet. Frank gave a sudden lurch forward, and brought one of the heavy jack-boots, smack, across Nero's nose.

And still Nero refused to move. He just stopped where he was, growling savagely.

And then, as Frank drew himself together for another smack at Nero, the pail on his head tipped, rolled off, and went clattering down the sewer, making a noise that echoed through the narrow tunnel like clap after clap of thunder. It was too much for Nero, he turned tail – and vanished!

Then they found out why the poor beast had refused to move before. Immediately behind him was an eight-foot fall in the sewer tunnel; and now, somewhere beyond this fall, they could hear him roaring, and roaring, and roaring! Scrambling down the eight-foot drop, they followed the sound, and very soon they found him. In leaping another fall he had caught his hind legs and quarters in one of the slip-nooses that had been lowered from a man-hole. And there he was, hanging upside down, and quite helpless.

Poor Nero! By means of other ropes they speedily managed to turn him right side up. The shifting den was fetched, and set in place above him. And so, wet, cold, covered with filth, and as unlike a king of beasts as anything could well be, they hauled him up, got him into the shifting den, and rushed him back to the menagerie. And there, on a huge bed of straw, with plenty of food and water close beside him, they left him to rest and recover, and clean himself up.

And Marco, the boarhound? Yes, he recovered from his wounds, so all ended happily.

22   God stood scratching his head and looking at it. Already it had crushed most of his carrots out of sight. If it went on growing at this rate it would soon be pushing his house over.

Suddenly, as he looked at it, it opened an eye and looked at him.

God was amazed.

The eye was quite small and round. It was near the thickest end, and farthest from the root. He walked round to the other side, and there was another eye, also looking at him.

'Well!' said God.'And how do you do?'

The round eye blinked, and the smooth glossy skin under it

wrinkled slightly, as if the thing were smiling. But there was no mouth, so God wasn't sure.

Next morning God rose early and went out into his garden.

Sure enough, during the night his new black plant with eyes had doubled its length again. It had pushed down part of his fence, so that its head was sticking out into the road, one eye looking up it, and one down. Its side was pressed against the kitchen wall.

God walked round to its front and looked it in the eye.

'You are too big,' he said sternly. 'Please stop growing before you push my house down.'

To his surprise, the plant opened a mouth. A long slit of a mouth, which ran back on either side under the eyes.

'I can't,' said the mouth.

God didn't know what to say. At last he said:

'Well then, can you tell me what sort of a thing you are? Do you know?'

'I,' said the thing, 'am Whale-Wort. You have heard of Egg-Plant, and Buck-Wheat, and Dog-Daisy. Well, I am Whale-Wort.'

There was nothing God could do about that.

By next morning, Whale-Wort stretched right across the road, and his side had pushed the kitchen wall into the kitchen. He was now longer and fatter than a bus.

When God saw this, he called the creatures together.

'Here's a strange thing,' he said. 'Look at it. What are we going to do with it?'

What do you think the creatures answered?

23   'Yes, why not? You found it. Though I suppose we ought to give it to the Museum.'

'No, no! You won't really? – Please let me have it. It's my special want.'

'Yes, I said you could have it. We'll give the negative to the Museum.'

All afternoon Rob helped his father to load stones onto a trolley and wheel them to the site of the wall. After tea they drove round to the Museum, taking both fossil stones to show the Director. The larger, heavier piece held the hollow shape, the actual fossil lay on a thin slab. Rob could easily carry it in his satchel.

At the office just inside the Museum door there was a tousled-looking young man with back street manners.

'Good afternoon,' said Rob's father. 'Where is my old friend Mr Porter? I hope he is not ill. Are you standing in for him?'

'He's retired. It's me now. What d'you want?'

'We would like to speak to the Director, please.'

'He's busy. You'll have to wait.'

'Will you tell him please that we are here? We'll wait in the fossil room. Come on, Rob. Let's go and see what fossils they have already. I'll be surprised if there is anything as good as ours. You could leave your satchel here in the office. It's heavy.'

Rob gave one look at the young Curator and decided he'd sooner carry it.

They went into the gallery where the fossils were on show, case after case with minute pieces of black stone displayed behind glass. The young man having telephoned through to the Director followed them in, sticking close to them and listening to everything they said as if they might be thieves. Rob was hopping about in excitement.

'They haven't got anything nearly as good as ours.'

His father pointed to a flat slab of stone covering most of a wall.

'What about that?' he said. In the middle of it, made while the rock was still hot and soft, was an immense print of a kind of hand, fantastic and horrible. The label underneath read,

Footprint of Megatherium

'Help!' said Rob. 'What's that?'

'It's a giant beast. I don't know what it was, but it bounded across hot rock.'

'It may be bigger than ours,' said Rob, 'but it's not as good. It's not a fossil at all.'

At this point the Director came into the gallery to look for them. He knew Rob's father well.

'Yes, it's sad that we have lost old Porter. This is his nephew, Stephen, who we hope will learn to take his place. Actually, this is his first day, so he hasn't acquired the Institutional mannerisms yet.' (A funny way, thought Rob's father, to say he is a lout.) 'He's got a thing about fossils; that's really what got him the place. I hope he'll learn to appreciate the rest in time. It takes time.'

'We have brought a fossil to show you, and another, not quite so good I'm afraid, to offer you. We left that one in the car because it's very heavy.

This was Rob's moment. He brought out his fossil snake and showed it to the Director. The young Curator's eyes showed white all round the iris like a madman's, and his enthusiasm overrode his manners so that he nosed in and jogged the Director's elbow.

'Careful, Stephen! You nearly made me drop it. My word! It is a beauty. We had better go into my study. Rob and I will go ahead, and perhaps you and Stephen will go and fetch the larger piece.'

In the study the Director hummed and got out large catalogues of other museums one after another, flipping over pages, saying after each one,

'No; no; no Ah! No.'

When the other two returned carrying the stone with the hollow shape, he greeted them with the information, 'There was one found in a quarry near Mousehole in 1884 – let me see, where is it now?'

'Minneapolis Museum,' prompted Stephen.

'Thank you, Stephen – I told you it was his subject – well now, Stephen, what do you think of these?'

Stephen swallowed hard. 'Fine,' he said.

The Director was extremely happy to accept the hollow stone. He asked what quarry it came from, what firm had supplied it, and what did they intend to do with the rest of the load. Then very gently but with overwhelming earnestness he suggested that the Museum ought to have both.

'You perhaps don't realize how rare these fossils are. Particularly the one your son has. Do you think it wise to entrust it to him? Boys are so careless.'

Stephen put out his hand to it but Rob snatched it up off the table and hugged it to him, looking anxiously at his father.

'You gave it me,' he said.

His father hesitated while Rob held his breath.

'I couldn't be so mean as to take it back when I've given it him.'

'Perhaps the young gentleman will be so generous as to give it us himself?' said the Director, smiling persuasively.

Rob looked imploringly at his father.

'It's my greatest treasure,' he said.

'I should think it is,' said the Director. 'It is worth a great deal of money, and has even more scientific value.'

Stephen turned to Rob.

'Look here,' he said, 'suppose I gave you ten pounds for it. Would that make a difference?'

What happened next?

24   It wasn't a gang really. I mean they didn't have meetings or anything like that. They just went around together wearing their balaclavas, and if you didn't have one you couldn't go round with them.

Tony and Barry were my best friends, but because I didn't have a balaclava, they wouldn't let me go round with them. I tried.

'Oh go on, Barry, let us walk round with you.'

'No, you can't. You're not a Balaclava Boy.'

'Oh go on.'

'No.'

I wasn't half fed-up. All my friends were in the Balaclava Boys. All the lads in my class except me. Wasn't fair.

The bell went for the next lesson – handicraft. I didn't half find handicraft class boring. I was just no good at handicraft and Mr Garnett agreed with me.

Today was worse than ever. We were painting pictures and we had to call it 'my favourite story'. Tony was painting *Noddy in Toyland*. I told him he'd get into trouble.

'Garnett'll do you.'

'Why? It's my favourite story.'

'Yes, but I don't think he'll believe you.'

Tony looked ever so hurt.

'But honest. It is my favourite story. Anyway, what are you doing?'

He leaned over to have a look at my favourite story.

'What is it?'

'It's *Robinson Crusoe* – what do you think it is?'

He just looked at my painting.

'Oh, I see it now. Oh yes, I get it now. I couldn't make it out for a minute. Oh yes, there's Man Friday behind him.'

'Get your finger off – it's still wet. And that isn't Man Friday, it's a coconut tree. And you've smudged it.'

We were using poster paint, and I got covered in it. I was getting it everywhere, so I asked Mr Garnett if I could go for a wash.

The wash-basins were in the boys' cloakroom just outside the main hall. I got most of the paint off, and as I was drying my hands that's when it happened.

What do you think did happen?

25   They were coming straight at him – at the pond! Couldn't they *see*? Surely they'd swerve. They'd stop short . . .

'Look out!' Jimmy cried.

On and on came the toboggan.

'Slow down,' Jimmy croaked.

At that pace and with that weight and given the three foot drop down to him he knew the sledge would shatter the pond like glass. He could see an explosion of ice on impact with cracks cobwebbing over the whole surface, reaching him even. Would they all be drowned?

'Please!' he bleated.

Still the toboggan came on.

'You'll break it!' he screeched. 'You'll break it!'

Already it was too late. He saw the toboggan reach a peak of speed at the pool's edge and rocket into the air. In a commotion of snow it clattered onto the pond's surface spilling Teddy and Kit and Pete on either side like a bronco bucking three riders at once.

'You'll break it,' Jimmy whispered.

And break it they had. But not the ice. Where the sledge had landed Jimmy saw the concrete base of the pool.

Why could he see it, and what does this mean?

---

26   Snakes he thought, like anything else, probably have favourite lairs. Where more likely than a warm dark place near the stone that had held it? He took his flashlight and lay down on the floor to look under the radiator. Curled up at the back against the wall was a bronze coloured snake, rather fatter than it had been as a fossil. Near it, where the pipe went down through the floor, was a hole that it could have squeezed through. It blinked sleepily at Rob and it did not occur to him to be afraid of it. It was his snake, and he had warmed it back to life. He was the companion of its lair. He hoped it would stay where it was and sleep off its first hunt after a million years. He wished he could freeze it up again when necessary, because it would never do for anyone else to see it.

27

'No it won't,' said God. 'But some of you will come out. Now just you start blowing some of yourself out through that hole.'

Whale-Wort blew, and a high jet of spray shot up out of the hole that God had made.

'Now go on blowing,' said God.

Whale-Wort blew and blew. Soon he was quite a bit smaller. As he shrunk, his skin, that had been so tight and glossy, became covered with tiny wrinkles. At last God said to him:

'When you're as small as a cucumber, just give a shout. Then you can come back into my garden. But until then, you shall stay in the sea.'

And God walked away with all his creatures, leaving Whale-Wort rolling and blowing in the sea.

Soon Whale-Wort was down to the size of a bus. But blowing was hard work, and by this time he felt like a sleep. He took a deep breath and sank down to the bottom of the sea for a sleep. Above all, he loved to sleep.

When he awoke he gave a roar of dismay.

Why do you think that Whale-Wort was dismayed: what had happened?

28

And whatever he did Jimmy wasn't going to hurry it. He sat on the stone surround of the pond and touched the ice with his toecap. It seemed firm enough. But that was near the edge. Did it get thicker or thinner at the centre? They'd also talked about that in the lesson but Jimmy couldn't remember what was said. Perhaps he should stay on the outside of the pond this first time . . .

No. That would be chicken. He had to cross it. Gingerly, sitting on the pond's edge, he lowered both feet onto the surface. Still firm. Supporting his weight with his hands he shifted to his knees then let go and eased forward . . . slowly, slowly . . . until he lay full-length stretched out like a starfish. From beneath him came a sound like the crunching of tiny egg shells. But that was just the snow on top of the ice, surely. Perhaps he should leave the next move until tomorrow.

a) *Do you think he did?*
b) *If so, what happened next?*
c) *If not, what did he do?*

29   I had to get rid of it. I went outside and put it down the lavatory. I had to pull the chain three times before it went away.

I could hardly eat my tea.

'What's wrong with you? Aren't you hungry?'

'No, not much.'

'What have you been eating? You've been eating sweets, haven't you?'

'No, I don't feel hungry.'

'Don't you feel well?'

'I'm all right.'

I wasn't. I felt terrible.

'Well, it's my bingo night, so make yourself some cocoa before you go to bed.'

I was scared stiff when I went to school next morning. In assembly it seemed different.

All the boys were looking at me. Norbert Lightowler pushed past and didn't say anything.

When prayers finished, the headmaster said he had something very important to announce – and I could feel myself going red. My ears were burning like anything and I was going hot and cold both at the same time.

'I'm very pleased to announce that the school football team has won the inter-league cup . . .'

And that was the end of assembly.

At playtime I could see all the Balaclava Boys going round together – and then I saw Norbert Lightowler was one of them.

'Have you bought a new one then, Norbert?'

'What?'

'You've bought a new balaclava, have you?'

'What are you talking about?'

'Your balaclava. You've got a new balaclava, haven't you?'

Norbert answered briefly and that is the end of the story. What do you think he said?

128